CRODA ADHESIVES
TECHNICAL LIBRARY

DATE   1970

ORIGINATOR   JB/AWO

REF NO.   14.13

a handbook of paperboard and board
its manufacturing technology, conversion and usage

A

Volume one
Manufacturing Technology

a handbook of

paperboard and board

its manufacturing technology,
conversion and usage

ROBERT R. A. HIGHAM

Business Books Limited *London*

First published 1970

© 1970 ROBERT R. A. HIGHAM

ISBN 0 220 99218 5

This book has been set in 10 on 11 pt Baskerville
and printed litho by R. MacLehose & Co. Ltd., Glasgow,
for the publishers, Business Books Limited
(registered office: 180 Fleet Street, London, E.C.4.),
publishing offices: Mercury House, Waterloo Road,
London, S.E.1.

MADE AND PRINTED IN GREAT BRITAIN

acknowledgements

The author wishes to record his grateful thanks to the following persons and organizations for supplying and for permission to reproduce the figures listed below, and to the many others who have been kind enough to personally or anonymously supply information and illustrations incorporated in this book.

Aktieselskabet De forenede Papirfabrikker, Fig. 1.18, ☐ Bertrams Ltd, England, Figs. 3.13, 3.19, 3.15, 3.16(a), 3.16(b), 3.19, 3.20 ☐ Billeruds Aktiabolag, Sweden, Figs. 1.4, 1.5, 1.6, 1.7, 1.24, 2.2, 2.8, 3.54, 4.10, 4.11, 4.14 ☐ Black Clawson International, Figs. 1.30, 1.31, 1.32, 1.33, 3.43, 3.44, 4.81(a), 4.4(b), 4.4(c), 4.4(d), 4.12 ☐ B.P.B.M.R.A., UK, Figs. 1.23 ☐ Defibrator Ltd, Sweden, Figs. 1.19, 1.20 ☐ Dorries GmbH, Germany, Figs. 3.4, 3.11 ☐ Federation Européen Des Fabricants De Carton Ondulé, and ASSCO Fiberboard Case Code, P. A. Gartaginis & H. J. Ostrowski ☐ H. W. Giertz & T. Lobben ☐ Iggesunds Bruk, Sweden, Figs. 4.1, 4.5, 4.13, 4.15 ☐ Karlstads Mekaniska Werkstad, Sweden, Figs. 3.55, 3.56, 3.57 ☐ Kobayàshi Engineering Works Ltd, Japan, Figs. 3.22(a), 3.22(b), 3.23, 3.24 ☐ Manchester Machinery Co. USA, Fig. 3.46 ☐ Dr. Hans Meyer, Fig. 1.8 ☐ Oy Keskuslaboratorio Centrallaboratorium AB, Finland, Fig. 3.25(c) ☐ Oy Tampella AB, Figs. 3.12, 3.17, 3.18, 3.35, 3.36, 3.37, 3.38, 3.39, 3.40, 3.41, 3.48(a), 3.48(b), 4.3, 4.8 ☐ The Institute of Paper Chemistry, USA, Figs. 1.11(a), 1.11(b), 2.4, 2.5, 2.6, 3.25(a), 3.25(b), 3.25(d) ☐ United States Department of Agriculture Forest Service, Figs. 1.9(a), 1.9(b), 1.21(a), 1.21(b), 3.1(a), 3.1(b), 3.1(c), 3.1(d), 3.2(a), 3.2(b), 3.2(c), 3.2(d) ☐ Veb Papiermaschinenwerke E. Germany, Figs. 3.7, 3.8 ☐ Waldron-Hartig Div., Midland-Ross Corp., USA, Fig. 4.6 ☐ Warmsleys, UK, Fig. 3.47 ☐ Weyerhaeuser Company, USA, Figs. 1.1, 1.2, 1.3, 2.3

To the following individuals the author would especially like to extend his considerable gratitude and thanks for their great kindness in contributing valuable help and information and for reading various chapters and sections throughout this book. Messrs J. S. Buchanan, Thames Board Mills Ltd, D. J. Fahey, J. W. Konig, jr, F. A. Simmonds, Forest Products Laboratory, Forest Service, US Department of Agriculture, D. Jarman, Masson Scott Thrissel Engineering Ltd, J. Moore, Fibreboard Packaging Case Manufacturers Association, J. Smart, Consolidated Papers Inc.

contents

Fibrous raw materials, plant fibres, "softwood", "hardwood"—Principles of chemical pulping, hemicelluloses and lignin—Fibre form, stress/strain characteristics—Pulp yield, active and passive fibres, modulus of elasticity, middle lamella, extensional stiffness—Lignin/hemicelluloses effect on pulps, delignification and carbohydrate degradation, DP, kraft and sulphite pulps—Influence of pulp quality on fluting medium properties—Effect of yield on strength properties, fibre flexibility, wet pressing, thermo-softening, increased bonding, elongation at rupture, fluting medium—Semichemical pulping principles, advantages of—Semichemical processes, "cold soda" process—Agricultural residues pulping processes, mechano-chemical process, Celdecor-pomilio, Soda/chlorine process, semi-chemical process—NSSC pulp process, hardwoods, fluting medium strength characteristics—Pandia process, 100% straw fluting, typical straw fluting strength properties—Peadco process, 70% bagasse fluting, Defibrator horizontal digester—HF-method for straw fluting—Simon-Cusi process, bagasse fibres, location of, process stages, depithing, chemical impregnation, continuous digestion, fractionation, semichemical and semi-mechanical pulping stages, full chemical pulping—Refiner chemical pulp—Thermomechanical pulping–Birch fibre, fibre length, fibre width, short fibres, pine fibres, "formation pulps", bonded network, long fibres, wet-web strength—The rôle of birch pulp in paperboards, single fibre strength—NSSC birch pulp for fluting, fibrillation, refining pulps together, fibre shortening—Birch pulp in kraft linerboard, in folding carton board, food board—Modern chemical pulp production techniques for fluting medium—Swedish mill practice, cross recovery—Finnish mill practice, ammonia based digestion, vapour phase—Japanese mill practice—Dutch mill practice.

Waste paper (paperstock) recovery, economic importance—De-inked waste, thermo-chemical reaction, de-inking chemicals, zinc hydrosulphite, sodium peroxide, sodium silicate — De-inking methods, washing, flotation—Flotation de-inking, groundwood and woodfree de-inking system, operational details, separation of printing ink, importance of pH in de-inking, groundwood, woodfree, power consumption—Processing equipment, modern Hydrapulper, ragger, junk remover, flote purge, pernicious contraries—Accessory defibring equipment, centrifugal disintegrating equipment, Hydrapulper vokes rotor—Deflakers or fiberizers, Escher Wyss deflaker, Scott-Rietz durafiner—Typical mill wastepaper systems, for removing all known evident contraries, typical woodfree de-inking system—Pernicious contraries in waste paper—European waste paper nomenclature, prohibited materials, improper materials or contaminants, European list of standard waste paper qualities.

Major stock preparation processes—refining, potential bonding, fibrous raw materials—Object of refining and refining principles, imbibition, fibre surfaces, mechanical entanglement, web consolidation, wet pressing, formation, fibre structure, intermediate drying, microfibril cohesion, hornification, mechanical flexion—Effects of refining on fibre structure—Fibril arrangement, drying tensions—ability of fibres to fibrillate, internal fibrillation, water absorption, fibre plasticity and flexibility—Effect of pulp properties on refining, morphological, physical, chemical, physiochemical, fibre strength, surface, length, cell wall thickness, hardwoods, softwoods, fibre form, pulp yield, passive and active segments, conformability, stress/strain, modulus of elasticity, cellulose purity, DP, sulphite, sulphate, fibre structural modification, hemicellulose, lignin, swollen condition of fibres, wetting—Exposed fibre wall surface, drying, primary and secondary walls (P & S$_1$)—Developments in stock preparation systems, UK and Europe, USA, integration, waste paper economics, slushing—Modern stock preparation methods, refining, hydration, "brushing", cutting—Refiner requirements, flexibility and versatility, cone and disc—Refiner variables, fibre toughness, high yield, softwood, hardwood, bar-to-bar pressure, fibre breakdown—Refiner tackle, fluid mechanics, fibre dewatering, elastic limit, flexure, reimbibition, "floc"—Refiner variables and quality considerations, flow rate, consistency, control techniques—Disc refiners, pulp load-carrying ability, freeness drop, disc "backing-off", disc refiner types and sizes, refiner bars, "hold-back or throw-out", burst and tear strength, disc plate configuration, linerboard, Jordan refiner, freeness—Linerboard stock refining in N. America

Terminology, paperboard, paper, board, "cardboard", container board, boxboard, folding boxboard, special foodboard, setup (rigid) boxboard, building board, tube board, fibreboard, corrugated, solid—Sheet formation—factors affecting it, headbox conditions, stock consistency, fibre form, pulp yield, fibre structure/form and exposed surface, bonding potential, technological factors related to formation—Development underlying modern boardmaking machines, N. America, Europe, Fourdrinier, secondary fibres, Fourdrinier combined machines, cylinder, notable machinery developments, Inverform, Ultra former, Verti-Forma, Papriformer—Boardmaking operations/methods, cylinder boards, existing wet processes, dry boardmaking, "after-processes"—Modern forming methods, multi-ply webs, Fourdrinier machine, cylinder, formers, double-wire drainage devices—multi-vat board machines, contraflow vat, uniflow vat, intermittent board machine, millboard, modified approach flow vats, Rotiformer, high freeness, sheet profile, ply bonding, heavy boards, weight profile, dry vat, formation, speed, Tampella dry vat, adjustable dry vat cylinder machines, formation, Tampella suction former, Versa vat, Stevens former, formation, hydraulic formers, board grain, Ultra former, stock flow, water removal, gravure, ply bond, stiffness, "combination" machines, interesting and unusual arrangements—Disadvantage of Fourdrinier principle, drainage hydrodynamics, Inverform, water removal, Inverform operation, boxboard, freeness, moisture content, operating factors, "square sheet", grain ratio, top liner applied at last station, reserve press—**Verti**-Forma—Papriformer—Multi-former—Board machine press section; object of, pressure, sheet consolidation, wet pressing, fibre elastic resistance and plastic conformability, removal of water—Different types of presses, fabric press, moisture content, shrink fabric press, method of water removal, Venta-nip press, arrangement for multi-ply board machine, UNI-press, pick-up, sheet transfer, fluting medium, kraft linerboard, "closed" transfer of sheet, UNI-press and fabric press—Typical paperboard mills in Europe, Australia, Fourdrinier/Inverform, carton board, corrugated and solid fibreboard, Denmark; Fourdrinier, straw pulp, fluting, Italy; Fourdrinier/cylinder, boxboards, refiners, Scotland; Inverform, chipboard, top liner at first station, Spain; Fourdrinier/cylinder, box-board and container boards, Inverform—Paperboard machine specifications (Table), Fourdrinier/cylinder units in eight countries (Table).

Reasons for coating, printable clay-type coatings, functional coating, barrier coating properties—Board surface properties—Board mechanical characteristics—Main requirements of paperboards for coating—Selecting a coating material, binders in common use—Functional coating and/or laminating—Important properties of functional coatings and their benefits, grease resistance, moisture vapour resistance, gas and odour resistance, heat resistance, water resistance, chemical resistance, wet strength, dry sheet-strength—Functional coating materials, PVDC, polyethylene, paraffin wax, microcrystalline wax, hot melts—Effect of rheological properties of coatings—Coating practice and machine developments—"On"-machine coating—Multi-station coating—Blade/airknife coating—Blade-on-blade coating—Four-stage multi-coating—Size press and precoating devices—"Off"-machine coating develop-ments—Online coating arrangements—Coating methods "on"-machine—Size press pigment coating, "wash" coating, size press designs—Airknife coaters—Metering bar coaters—Rod coaters—Blade coaters—Pond-type (puddle)—Trailing-blade—Flexiblade—Flooded nip—Controlled fountain—Champflex coater—Combined "On"- or "Off"-machine coating arrangements—"Off"-machine coating methods, coated wood pulp board grades, coated waste fibre board grades—Coating methods—"Off"-machine—Drying.

preface

WHILE IT IS true that most of the early history of the development of *paper* occurred in Europe, it is also true that the development of *paperboard* took place principally in the United States. Thus, at the end of the nineteenth century, paper was well established in the USA and Europe, but paperboard was really still in its infancy. Significant is that it took nearly 100 years before paperboard from straw pulp was made on a Fourdrinier machine. Yet paper from straw pulp was commonplace. Perhaps this is a clear enough indication that the problems encountered in the manufacture of paper and paperboard are quite distinctive. They are quite distinct industries which merely happen to have many aspects in common.

The subject of "paperboard and board", unlike "papermaking", appears to receive generally less emphasis at the current time in the technical literature. This probably also is reflected in the scarcity of reference books on the subject.

For some years a growing need has been expressed for a reference book tailored to the needs of technical management—a work that would selectively cover the important technological aspects of a broadly based paperboard industry, yet generally within the terms of reference such as under this title.

As with the author's treatment of "papermaking" in the sister volume of this work, *A Handbook of Papermaking*, the aim in these two volumes is to cover basically the technology of paperboard and board manufacture, its conversion and usage.

In recognizing that a single treatment cannot possibly attempt to be "all-things-to-all-men", the author has endeavoured to temper the degree of selectivity of subject matter in the light of the growing vertical integration taking place in the pulp, paper and board making industries on a world scale.

Thus, particular emphasis is focused on paperboard raw material aspects; on boardmaking technology, techniques and processes; on paperboard as a finished product as manifest in its conversion into corrugated board, etc., and in its performance properties; in paperboard component and package testing methods and relationships of these results to box and carton performance; and in the "nature" and end-usage of paperboard grades, materials and packages.

In deploring the absence of an index in too many technology books published in recent years, effort has been spent in providing a comprehensively cross sectioned index which complements the numerous sub-headings and plentiful cross references noted in the text.

February 1969   R.R.A.H.

paperboard fibrous raw materials chemical and semichemical pulping—secondary fibre materials

1

1.1 fibrous raw materials

It is not the author's aim in this section to cover more than a brief introduction to the fibrous raw materials used in the manufacture of papers and paperboards. The subject is comprehensively covered in a sequel edition to this volume under the title *A Handbook of Papermaking—the technology of pulp, paper and board manufacture*, Second Edition, 1968, by the author, and in other books. Therefore treatment here is limited to an understanding sufficient to place the subject into perspective in relation to the points discussed in the various chapters.

1.1.1 *Plant fibres*

In the plant, woody cells are formed during active growth. The most important of these from a paper and board maker's consideration are the fibres—a general term for a narrow elongated cell with tapering ends. A normal fibre is made up from several thicknesses of cell wall.

As is to be expected, the fibres of "softwoods", Figs. 1.1, 1.3, and 1.4, and "hardwoods", Figs. 1.2 and 1.5, differ appreciably. Softwoods have somewhat longer and broader fibres than hardwoods. The latter are characterized by the presence of large vessel-elements; often these are barrel-

Figure 1.1–1.3.   MICROGRAPHS OF WOOD FIBRES

Figure 1.1.   Spruce has both thin and thick fibres of average length 2·7 mm.

shaped, usually with thin walls and sometimes with perforations and spiral thickenings, Fig. 1.3. In birch wood, for example, these cells can be some ten times as wide as the fibres and amount to 20–25% by volume, Figs. 1.11(b). They contribute little if any "papermaking" value.

From the aspect of chemical composition, the cell wall of a fibre may be described as a division of two regions—namely, the compound, *middle lamella* and the secondary wall, Fig. 1.8. The middle lamella is comprised of lignin and hemicelluloses, while the secondary wall represents the cellulose carbohydrate fraction.

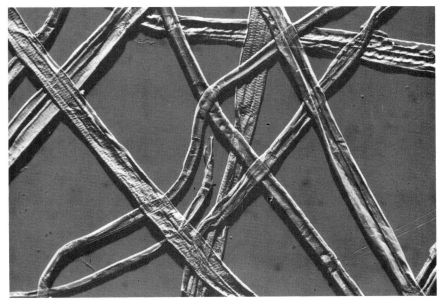

Figure 1.2.   Alder has a mixture of fibre lengths and sizes. Note the presence of the large bulbous cell typical of hardwoods. Average fibre length is 1·2 mm.

The development of most paper and board properties is influenced by fibre wall thickness and cell formation. Pulps most suitable for papermaking are produced from cells with thin walls. This is because thin walled fibres produce a dense, more evenly formed sheet compared with papers made with thick walled fibres that give bulky (large air space), coarse textured papers. In the case of paperboards, owing to their "heavier" construction, the foregoing probably has less influence in terms of single, sheet properties.

1.2 chemical pulping principles

Chemical pulping—cooking or digestion—of raw materials for paper and board making involves an initial breaking down of the fibrous raw material, either in the cooking process alone or by a combination of cooking and bleaching stages. During processing, hemicellulosic and ligneous binding materials are removed to an extent varying with the type and severity of the cooking conditions prevailing, leaving behind the "purified" cellulose fibres. These are afterwards washed free of digestion chemicals.

Chemical pulping processes consist of three important steps:

1 Diffusion of the cooking liquor into the plant tissue.
2 Reaction of the liquor with lignin, etc.
3 Diffusion of the dissolved constituents out of the raw material.

Provided the temperature is high enough, the limiting factor in the cooking process is the speed of diffusion of the liquor.

1.2.1 *Fibre form*

Fibre form is important as it is influential in the development of stress/strain characteristics in the formed sheet. Fibre form is dependent on pulp yield. Low yield pulps are characterized by their thin, curled, bent and kinked fibres, Fig. 1.4. In addition, and particularly with acid sulphite pulp, many fibres appear broken and fragmented. Strong sulphite and ordinary kraft pulps produce somewhat straighter and less fragmented fibres, although still curled and kinked in appearance, Fig. 1.5. Bisulphite (high yield) and semichemical pulps produce thick relatively straight fibres, Fig. 1.6. Ordinary bisulphite and modified kraft, swollen pulps fall between high yield bisulphite and ordinary kraft. For contrast Fig. 1.7 illustrates groundwood.

Figure 1.3.   Fir has longer fibres, average length 3·5 mm. Noticeable is the difference between springwood and summerwood fibres—the former show spiral thickenings.

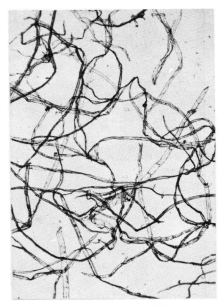

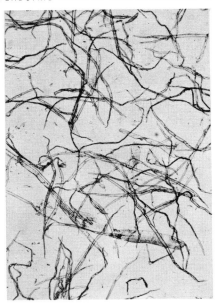

Figure 1.4.   SPRUCE SULPHITE FIBRES

Fibre form is dependent on pulp yield—low yield pulps are characterized by their thin, curled, bent and kinked fibres.

Figure 1.5.   BIRCH SULPHATE FIBRES

Ordinary kraft pulps produce somewhat straighter and less fragmented fibres, although still curled up and kinked in appearance.

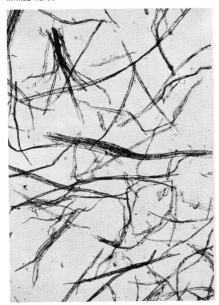

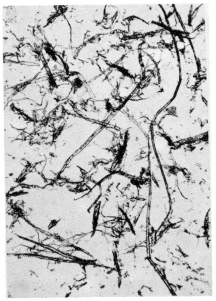

Figure 1.6.   BIRCH SEMICHEMICAL FIBRES

Semichemical processed pulps produce thick, relatively straight fibres.

Figure 1.7.   SPRUCE GROUNDWOOD

Provides a contrast with chemical pulps.

When analysing the influence of fibre form on paper strength properties, reference should be made to the concept of *passive* and *active* fibre segments. According to this, the great differences in the modulus of elasticity of different papers/boards are, at least partly, a consequence of the number of fibres actually stressed when the sheet is loaded. If the modulus of elasticity is low, this is an indication that much of the fibrous material is not taking part in the load-carrying mechanism—that is, some segments are passive. They have for one reason or another not been stretched when the sheet was dried and they are not being stressed when it is loaded.

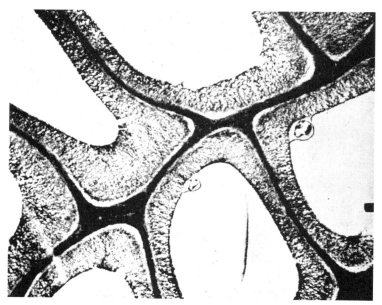

Figure 1.8.   IN CHEMICAL PULP PROCESSES, INITIAL SEPARATION OF FIBRES OCCURS IN THE TRUE MIDDLE LAMELLA.

In chemical pulp processes, initial separation of the fibres takes place in the true middle lamella, Fig. 1.8. But in some semichemical processes, e.g., the cold soda process, initial separation occurs between the outer and middle layers of the secondary fibre wall, Fig. 1.9(a)(b). On refining chemical pulps, the basic change in fibre structure seems to involve the successive removal of lamellae from the outer layer of the secondary wall. It has been shown that in pulps refined to a degree beyond that carried out commercially, the layer $S1$ is substantially intact. With semichemical pulps, however, the region external to the middle layer of the secondary fibre wall separates on refining as a single structural complex, so that the exposed surfaces of such fibres and the *fines* produced differ morphologically from those of chemical pulps. Thus, the bonding of fibres of semichemical pulps could arise between surfaces of very different composition and physical organization.

High yield bisulphite pulp has straight and highly swollen fibres. As a consequence, they form strong and bulky sheets. The paper/board has high

Figure 1.9(a) and (b). IN SOME SEMICHEMICAL PULPS, INITIAL FIBRE SEPARATION OCCURS BETWEEN THE OUTER AND MIDDLE LAYERS OF THE SECONDARY FIBRE WALL.

extensional stiffness* and high tensile strength even when unrefined or slightly beaten. This indicates that most segments have been activated without refining. Further refining will increase the strength only slightly. Low yield pulps with curved, kinked and slightly swollen fibres need beating in order to shorten the average segment length for increased bonding. For unrefined pulps, a close correlation exists between extensional stiffness and hemicellulose content. As a consequence of high bulk and high extensional stiffness, paper/boards made from high yield pulps may be expected to exhibit high bonding stiffness—Fig. 1.10.

1.2.2 *Lignin—effect on pulps*

The hydrophobic character of lignin largely counteracts bonding. Delignification thus improves paper strength and decreases opacity, from the mechanical, through the semichemical to the chemical pulping region, where the strength properties have a maximum. The maximum arises from the secondary effect of carbohydrate damage on continued delignification to low lignin contents.

The nature of the pulping chemicals will influence the properties of the residual lignin (see section 1.5), but still more so of the residual carbohydrates. It affects the selectivity of delignification, of carbohydrate removal (hemicelluloses, etc.) and of carbohydrate degradation. The quantity rather than the chemical nature of hemicelluloses appears to determine the sheet properties. The quality of the hemicelluloses may play a role, since kraft pulp

---

The extensional stiffness, in contrast to the modulus of elasticity, is not based on a certain cross-area, but on a strip of "paper" of certain width. It is reported as the force needed to obtain an elastic elongation of 100%. The extensional stiffness gives an indication of the amount of cellulose material actually carrying the load when the paper is loaded.

hemicelluloses have a higher DP than those in sulphite pulp. This may, however, just indicate a more or less uniform carbohydrate degradation, also of the cellulose microfibrils. The lateral order of these may be important, and it is noted that the lower yield of kraft pulps as compared to sulphite pulps is largely caused by removal of less-ordered cellulose.

The influence of the raw material can be largely assigned to the length and cell wall thickness of the fibres rather than to the chemical composition. Figures 1.11(a)(b) illustrate this difference.

When comparing pulps with the same hemicellulose content but different lignin content, sulphate and sulphite pulps should be kept separate. The

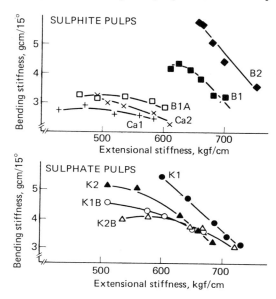

Type of woodpulp	Pulp yield, %	Lignin content, %	Hemi- cellulose content, %	Symbol in the graphs	
Soft sulphite	43	1	6	Ca1	+
Strong sulphite	48	2	12	Ca2	×
Bisulphite	53	6	15	B1	■
Bisulphite	59	11	18	B2	◆
Bleached and hot alkali-refined bisulphite B1	43	–	8	B1A	□
Sulphate	47	4	11	K1	●
Bleached sul- phate	44	–	10	K1B	○
Polysulphide	56	8	20	K2	▲
Bleached poly- sulphide	49	–	17	K2B	△

Figure 1.10. BENDING STIFFNESS OF PULPS PLOTTED AGAINST EXTENSIONAL STIFFNESS.

(a)

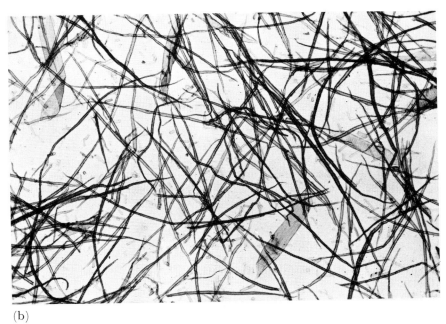

(b)

Figure 1.11.   INFLUENCE OF THE RAW MATERIAL PULP.
This can be largely assigned to length and cell wall thickness of the fibres, rather than to chemical composition.
These pictures illustrate this difference. They are of a species of softwood and a species of birch hardwood.

lignin in sulphate pulps is still of native, hydrophobic nature; with increased lignin content, the fibre becomes coarse and stiff, the pulp is difficult to beat and the paper is bulky with low strength. This is why kraft pulps of somewhat higher yield than ordinary are used only for kraft liner and that semichemical kraft pulps do not exist. In unbleached sulphite pulps, however, the lignin has been converted to solid lignin sulphonic acid, which is a highly hydrophilic and therefore swollen substance. It should be remembered that free lignin sulphonic acid is water soluble. From a paper bonding point of view, lignin in sulphite pulps might therefore be more or less compared with hemicellulose. High yield sulphite pulps, with high lignin content, are easy to beat and form very strong sheets.

For the production of pulps with very high yields (75–95%), cooking with bisulphite and neutral sulphite liquors seems to be of greatest interest, both because of pulp quality and colour. Depending on yield, the pulps can be largely grouped into two classes. Below a yield of about 80%, the chips are so softened that refining results in the separation of whole fibres. Such semi-chemical pulps form strong papers and resemble chemical pulps in their general properties. They are likely to increasingly be used to substitute un-bleached sulphite and kraft pulps.

In the yield range above 80%, the chips are still hard and defibration results in a mixture of whole fibres, fibre fragments and fines. The proportions among these fractions depend on cooking conditions, yield and refining conditions. Such pulps possess to a large extent the properties of mechanical pulps, but are stronger. Great efforts are paid today to the bleaching of such chemimechanical pulps and, if these efforts are successful, this new type of pulp will most probably be of great technical importance.

1.3 pulp yield

Pulp yield affects most paperboard properties; these properties in turn in-fluence converting efficiency. Table 1.1(a)(b) and Fig. 1.12 show the effect of yield on some strength properties of experimental semichemical fluting medium. As will be seen, within the range of typical semichemical pulp yields, the lower the yield, the better is the average dry-sheet strength. Most of the trends in pulp strength properties can be accounted for by an increase in flexibility and bonding of the fibres. This results in a progressively denser sheet with decreasing yield.

There exists a certain amount of disagreement in the conclusions arrived at by different workers in this field. As pointed out elsewhere, the probable reason for this apparent discrepancy is because a clear distinction must be made between the strength properties attributed to variation in yield achieved by wet pressing at the same yield and degree of refining in contrast to instances where variations in yield or refining time have taken place.

To repeat, it is important to keep in mind in dealing with high yield pulps that yield does not refer to an increase or decrease in quantity of fibres but to the presence of thermoplastic components such as lignin and hemicelluloses.

As percent yield decreases, mechanical properties including elongation, tensile strength and the energy required to break say a fluted sample improve

Table 1.1(a).   EFFECT OF YIELD ON SOME STRENGTH PROPERTIES OF
EXPERIMENTAL FLUTING MEDIUM

The effect of yield (a) on the lignin and pentosan content of typical US semichemical fluting medium pulps,
and (b) on some mechanical properties of handsheets made from these pulps. Unfluted samples.

Total % yield	Lignin %OD pulp	Pentosans %OD pulp	Con- ditioned Concora	Burst + ½ tear factor	Tensile strength Bl. Km.	Elongation %	Work to rupture ft lb/ft²
90·8	18·6	15·3	22·9	24	2·3	0·91	—
84·3	17·7	15·2	41·2	49	5·0	1·57	2·69
81·4	15·3	15·6	50·9	55	6·0	1·93	3·00
80·1	16·7	14·8	57·6	61	6·7	1·93	4·33
78·6	17·4	14·8	51·6	67	6·3	1·91	3·05
75·3	18·4	14·7	50·2	66	7·0	2·26	4·62
72·0	15·2	14·7	53·8	66	5·8	1·93	(2·92)
65·5	10·8	14·5	60·4	85	8·7	2·73	6·82

Table 1.1(b).   EFFECT OF YIELD ON LIGNIN AND PENTOSAN CONTENT OF
TYPICAL SEMICHEMICAL MEDIUM PULPS

%Yield	84·3	81·4	75·3	72·0	65·5
% Lignin	17·7	15·3	18·4	15·2	10·8
Work to stretch (ft lb ft²)	0·70	0·79	0·79	0·81	0·87
Work to break (ft lb ft²)	2·62	3·85	5·10	4·77	8·45
Tensile strength (Bl. Km.)	4·3	5·6	6·5	6·4	9·0

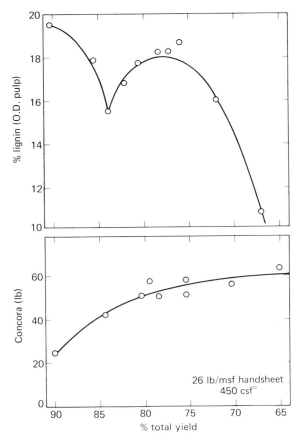

Figure 1.12.   EFFECT OF YIELD ON LIGNIN AND CONCORA VALUE OF SCCM PULP

rapidly. Significant in terms of a pulp's potential dry-sheet strength properties is that between yields of 90·8% and 65·5% pulp strength increases rapidly. At these yields lignin decreases from 18·6% to 10·8% OD pulp, whereas the hemicelluloses remain constant at around 15%.

It is probable that the presence of lignin plays an important rôle in the fluting operation in a corrugating machine, in terms of its thermosoftening properties and the hemicelluloses as they promote fibre bonds within the sheet. Increased bonding results in higher elongation at rupture. Low yield pulps, therefore, elongate more. Runnability of fluting medium also depends to an extent on tearing strength. This is similarly influenced by pulp yields.

1.4 influence of pulp quality on fluting medium

The type of pulp used in the manufacture of fluting medium has an important influence on strength properties—namely crushing strength.

In the main, virgin pulps used in fluting manufacture are of the semi-chemical type, with yields of some 55–80% made by a variety of cooking processes, from predominantly hard- and softwoods. Yield has actually no significant effect on ring crush strength.

It is known that the degree of refining significantly improves crushing strength, ring crush and flat crush. But this is true only over an optimum freeness range of 25–30° SR. Further refining reportedly has no effect on crush resistance.

Crushing resistance is related linearly to grammage, other conditions of pulp type and refining degree remaining equal. Stiffness of the paper increases with thickness (caliper). So does the force necessary to press the corrugations out of the sheet.

Typical figures for ring crush strength comparison of different fibrous furnishes indicate that beech monosulphite 74% yield pulp and spruce bisulphite pulp both gave some 200% higher ring crush compared with waste paper furnish. A mixture of 60% beech monosulphite and waste paper furnish is capable of giving a 120% improvement (1·5 kg/cm) on a 100% waste furnish alone.

1.5 semichemical pulping principles

It has been explained that during the chemical digestion process, lignin and some of the lower forms of cellulose, comprising other carbohydrates and hemicellulose fractions, are removed from the material. In practice, after the removal of these substances a pulp yield of only around 40–60% is generally obtained, the other materials present in the natural wood being lost from the point of view of fibrous stock.

The object of the semichemical processes is, therefore, to produce as high a pulp yield as possible commensurate with the best possible strength and cleanliness. Impregnation, cooking and defibrating techniques are of great importance in the semichemical processes. The pulp so obtained is suitable for grades such as: wrappings, newsprint, fluting medium, paperboards, etc.

In principle, semichemical processes produce high yields (ca. 75–83%) of unbleached pulp by a two stage method, involving in the first stage a mild chemical digestion and in the second mechanical disintegration. Pulp quality depends on the balance between these two treatments and on the type of raw material.

Generally, conventional type chemicals as used in chemical pulping are employed, e.g., caustic soda (NaOH), sodium bisulphite (Na_2SO_3), sodium carbonate (Na_2CO_3) or sulphate (Na_2SO_4) as a buffer to neutralize acids formed in the cooking process, sulphur (S), iron pyrites (Fe_2S), lime ($CaCO_3$), etc., plus chlorine-type bleaching agents for bleached grades. Ammonia base (ammonium sulphite) NSSC pulps are also finding favour, partly because the spent digestion liquor can be evaporated and burned. Although these are all alkaline processes—making possible the recovery of spent liquor—conditions of operation sometimes prevent economic soda recovery. Spent digestion liquors are therefore rejected as waste and create a major difficulty in effluent disposal.

Modern practice tends to link semichemical pulping processes to conventional kraft processes in order to make possible a cross recovery of the spent digestion liquors in the former process; see section 9.4.1. This solves both recovery problems for the NSSC mill and furnishes make-up chemicals for the kraft mill. For mills without this possibility, recovery is now feasible by using a new combination method of Stora's recovery system and a Broby furnace.

ADVANTAGES OF SEMICHEMICAL PULPING. Some of the main advantages are listed below:

Improved sheet formation characteristics. As a result of the higher yield, hemicelluloses mostly lost in conventional chemical digestion processes are retained to a greater degree and, therefore, an improved potential strength development characteristic in the pulp is obtained. Owing to the higher pulp yield, production costs are relatively lower. The ability to process many species of woods and also agricultural residues, e.g., bagasse, results in a wider availability of supply of materials.

The shorter process time factor and lower chemical cost improves the process economics and, owing to the high yield, material waste is reduced.

1.5.1 *Modern process methods*

Modern semichemical methods utilize continuous operation, which involves the use of special equipment. A notable and particular piece of equipment is the Pandia Chemipulper continuous digester.

1.5.2 *Pandia Chemipulper*

The Pandia process—see section 1.6.5—is a continuous process which readily lends itself to the recovery of spent cooking liquor as in the case of the NSSC process.

The principal element of the Pandia Chemipulper consists of one or more horizontal tubes joined by connecting links. Wood chips and/or other fibrous cellulosic material is moved continuously through these tubes by variable drive screw conveyance, along with the cooking liquor, and is digested at high temperature and pressure.

The number of tubes in an installation is governed by the type of raw material, the tonnage and by the cooking period required. Production capacity of Chemipulpers ranges from 25–300 tons per 24 hours.

The tubes are fed by screw feeder and discharge into the discharger. The screw feeder continuously feeds wood chips or other cellulosic material, at a constant rate, from the atmosphere into the pressure zone of the digester tubes. Its action is to "open up" the material, making rapid liquor impregnation possible.

The discharger passes the pulp from the pressure zone of the tubes to the atmosphere at a constant rate.

1.6 **semichemical processes**

"Cold" Soda process

The process was developed in the USA. Wood chips are steeped in warm caustic soda at atmospheric pressure (to open up the fibrous structure) and are then treated mechanically, e.g., refiners—much depends on this stage. Continuous operation is possible and the liquor can be re-used to some extent, although integration of the cold soda process with other pulping processes that incorporate soda recovery is preferable.

Good results are obtained with pulp yields of up to 90% using hardwoods (area of most importance for the cold soda process), particularly semi-tropical hardwoods and eucalyptus. Pulps obtained have poor bleachability, consequently the process is more suited to hardwoods—being more readily bleached. Typical cold soda pulps produce a sheet with high rattle, low bulk and opacity properties, owing to the higher proportion of hemicelluloses present.

Variations of the "cold" soda process involve treatment under $9 \cdot 8$ kg/cm^2 pressure (140 lb/in^2), shorter time cycles and weaker caustic liquor; also a so-called cold soda process at 40°C for 15 min.

The Kamyr method is used with pre-impregnation at $9 \cdot 9$ kg/cm^2 at 30–40°C, with 6–7 NaOH on oven dry weight of wood, with two stage disc refining, to produce an 82% yield of bleached pulp (peroxide and hydrosulphite at 70–75% G.E. brightness). The pulp is used mainly in coated and uncoated printing papers.

1.6.1 Agricultural residues pulping processes; for fluting

1.6.2 Mechano-chemical process

With this method of pulping, chopped straw or bagasse is defibred batchwise or continuously in open vessels, such as a Hydrapulper, using NaOH at atmospheric pressure and at a temperature of approximately 100°C for 30–50 min. Pulp consistency is about 10%, and sodium hydroxide of about 10–15% on weight of material is used to open up the plant structure.

Bleaching follows the pulping operation and involves a three stage process, e.g., chlorination–alkaline extraction–hypochlorite bleach. Pulp yields are considerably higher compared with conventional pressure digestion and may be in the region of 45–50% of bleached pulp, of 82–83 G.E., and 70% unbleached pulp, with the pulper running for 30–60 min. High yields are the attraction of the process, because of the high proportion of hemicelluloses. These pulps are particularly suitable for the manufacture of corrugating base papers. The principal disadvantage concerns difficult liquor recovery with its attendant effluent disposal problems.

1.6.3 *Celdecor-Pomilio soda/chlorine process*

In this process the operations of pulping and bleaching (when bleached pulp is required) can almost be regarded as one. In principle, chopped material is subjected to continuous caustic digestion in towers, followed by chlorination with chlorine gas at high pulp consistency, e.g., 30–35%. This is followed by alkaline extraction and hypochlorite bleaching.

This process is also useful for other agricultural residues and a flow diagram of operations is illustrated in Fig. 1.13.

The Celdecor continuous digester derives from the first successful continuous digester of any sort for pulp production. This was designed by the Pomilio brothers some 40 years ago. The process was conceived to work with an integrated electrochemical plant to produce the necessary caustic soda and chlorine. Most installations are so integrated. Thus, electrolysis of a solution of sodium chloride solution yields: $NaOH$, Cl_2 and H_2.

The process was originally applied to straw, but is equally suited to similar fibrous plants, of which bagasse (sugar cane waste) is currently most important—largely for economic reasons in developing countries deficient in forests.

As shown in Fig. 1.13, the process stages are: cutting of straw or disintegration of bagasse; dusting; pre-soaking (possible depithing of bagasse before soaking); dosing material by absorption with weak caustic soda and continuous discharge to digester top; cooking as material travels by controlled gravity down the direct steam and steam jacket heated tower; displacement washing out of black liquor on specially designed rotary vacuum filters. The semipulp is now ready for use in making coarse wrappers and container board grades, and is particularly suitable for corrugating medium. When used in this way, alkaline refining precedes washing. The pulp may be further screened if required for high grade wrappings, in which amounts up to 50% in a mixture with kraft wood pulp will not materially reduce sheet strength —proving its value as a secondary fibre supply.

The pulp may be satisfactorily bleached by single stage hypochlorite for use in bleached wrappers and *manillas*. For high grade bleached pulps the stages follow on from displacement washing, to dewatering in screw presses to about 30% consistency; opening or fluffing in a special machine to break up pressed material to a damp shag tobacco-like form; high consistency gas chlorination in gravity fed towers at low pH, which from the usual reaction by-product forms HCl. This being highly concentrated inhibits oxidation and promotes true chlorination to produce a superior strength pulp.

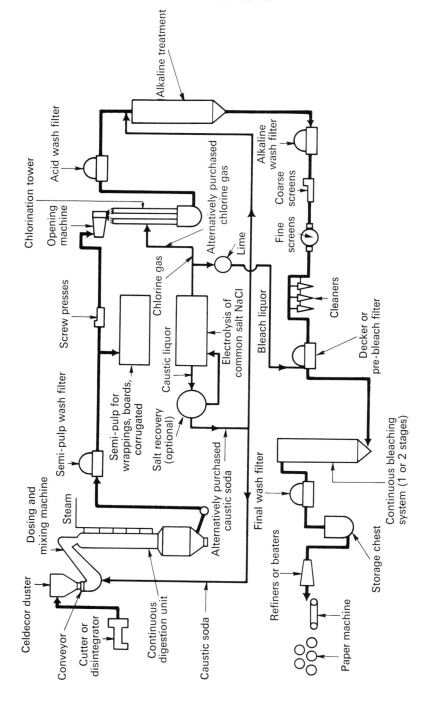

Figure 1.13.   CELDECOR-POMILIO PROCESS

1.6.4 Semichemical process

The semichemical process was first used in the USA in 1925. Today it is largely used in the production of hardwood pulps to which the process is ideally suited—giving yields between 60–80% for bleached and unbleached pulps respectively.

It is essentially a two stage process—the first stage consisting of mild chemical action to loosen and partly remove lignin—the second stage, a mechanical treatment involving use of defibrating equipment, e.g., disc refiners, disintegrators, classifiers, etc. Both acid and alkaline chemicals are and may be used, but the monosulphite process is more generally used for the first stage.

Also widely used is the (NSSC) *Neutral sulphite semichemical* process, especially in making corrugating base papers—fluting medium.

1.6.5 NSSC pulp process

The NSSC (neutral sulphite semichemical) pulping process is commonly applied in the manufacture of pulp for fluting medium. (Bleaching is difficult and requires a three stage process.)

It is common to use hardwoods of the alder, birch, maple variety. In Japan, elm, oak and willow are also used, and in France, poplar, hornbeam and beech. Interesting, is that one Japanese mill and a mill in France process *unbarked* wood in usual chip form. Bark not removed after screening from multiknife chippers, passes with the chips to the digester. Using vortex-type separators in the pulp mill and rotary cleaners ahead of the paper machine, it is possible to achieve 3–6% increase in pulp yield without sacrificing end product quality.

In the Japanese mill chips are cooked to approximately 80% yield, in a liquor consisting of 16% b.d. chipweight of sodium sulphite (Na_2SO_3) and 2·5% sodium carbonate (Na_2CO_3), at 180°C for 20 minutes. After digestion, pulp chips pass through high density liquor extraction to double disc refiners for primary fiberizing. Discharge is into large, agitated stock chests. Pulp is then screened on rotary screens and passed to double disc refiners for freeness control. Final freeness (fibre length) control is achieved in Jordan-type refiners.

Fluting medium produced in this manner exhibits the following strength characteristics: Grammage 130 g/m²; density 0·54; Burst 2·54 kg/cm²; Tensile (MD/CD) 7·1/4·5 kg; Tear (MD/CD) 90/110 g; Fold (MD/CD) 34/35 times (MIT 1 kg); Ring crush (MD/CD) 24/21 kg; Concora 23 kg.

In the French mill, cooking conditions are: 10·5% Na_2SO_3, 2% Na_2CO_3 at 175°C for 30 min, with a similar liquor to wood concentration and yield as the Japanese conditions.

1.6.6 Pandia process

The Pandia continuous digestion system is equally suitable for the processing of woods, Fig. 1.14 (see section 1.5.2), as well as other cellulosic

Pandia arrangement for hardwood or softwood cooking.

1. Pre-steamer
2. Screw feeder
3. Stop valve
4. Steam inlet
5. Pre-impregnating tube
6. Rotary valve
7. Digesting tube
8. Discharger
9. Blow valve
10. Blow pipes
11. Live bottom blow tank
12. Pulp to refiners
13. Make-up liquor
14. Re-circulating tank

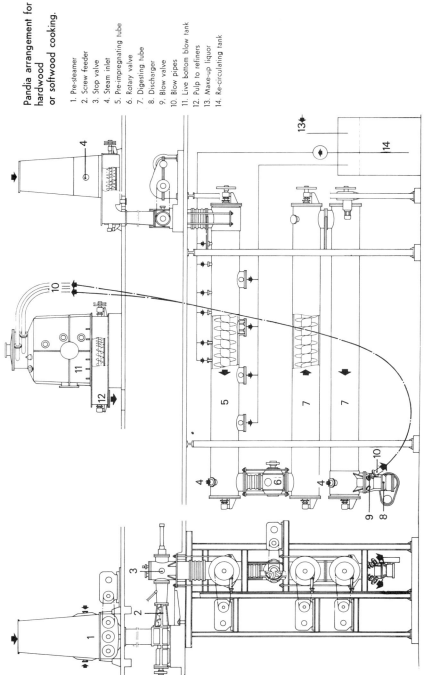

Figure 1.14.   PANDIA ARRANGEMENT FOR HARD AND SOFTWOOD COOKING

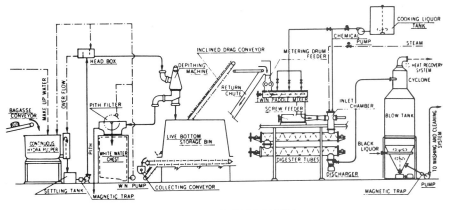

Figure 1.15.   PANDIA ARRANGEMENT FOR BAGASSE COOKING

Table 1.2.   TYPICAL STRENGTH FIGURES FOR STRAW PULP FOR FLUTING MEDIUM—
PANDIA PROCESS

	Tensile strength in Kg		Ring	
Basic weight	Machine	Cross	crush	CMT
gr/m^2	direction	direction	lb	lb
127	9·5	5·2	45	72
125	8·8	4·8	42	65
115	8·0	4·2	36	59
90	6·4	3·8	28	48

materials like straw, etc., Fig. 1.15. One large modern mill (in Greece) uses the Pandia process in the production of 100% straw pulp for fluting medium. Typical strength figures are shown in Table 1.2.

Dusted and chopped straw of about 5 cm in length is pneumatically conveyed to a straw bin ahead of the continuous digestion system. From here, it is fed into two horizontal, 1 m (42 in diameter) (35 ft) long digester tubes, by screw feeders. Through a rotating discharging device, the *brown-stock* is continuously blown to the blow tank.

Cooking time is about 8–10 min using the soda process. The cooking liquor is composed of caustic soda and black liquor from the wash plant. Straw to cooking liquor ratio is 1 : 3·5. Total active alkali, NaOH as Na_2O on straw is 4·75%. Digestion pressure is 7·5 kg/cm². Yield is 65%.

Brown-stock from the blow tank is continuously transferred to two *deckers* operating in series. Stock consistency is reduced to 2·5% to effect proper separation from the pulp of sand, grit and other extraneous materials in liquid cyclones. The deckers concentrate the stock to 5·5–6% consistency. It is then pumped to a 1 m (42 in) disc refiner for hot stock refining. Washing is conducted on a four stage, counter current liquor flow system employing hot water for the final phase.

1.6.7 *Simon-Cusi pulping process*

The Simon-Cusi process was developed exclusively for pulp and paperboard production from annual plant fibres, especially from bagasse (a by-product of cane sugar manufacture). The process is used for the production of a wide range of commercial papers and paperboards ranging from different grades of newsprint through a range of wrapping and sack papers, fluting medium and bleached paperboards to fine printings and writing.

As a single stage method of chemical pulping (as traditionally applied to wood), the process gives an unprofitably low yield—much of the softer fibre is destroyed by the chemicals in solutions.

The location of fibres in bagasse is not uniform—they range from a hard and lignified form to a soft and easily pulpable form. The Simon-Cusi process aims to remove the pith; to subject the fibre to initial light digesting in caustic soda; and then to separate the hard and soft fibres for different treatment. The soft fibres are in fact already pulped at this stage, whereas the hard fibres need a further mechanical or chemical treatment.

A number of variations are made possible in the system in order to produce a relatively wide range of quality pulps, from a single raw material source.

Variable process control over severity of depithing means that the average fibre length can be controlled. By varying the severity of initial digestion, so the quality and property of the pulp and fibre produced by fractionation can be controlled. Mechanical or chemical defibration methods of variable intensity can be used for second stage treatment of the harder fibres. Pulp fractions produced can be kept apart to give a two stream output or re-combined to give a single stream output. The individual pulp fractions can be bleached if required.

Thus, the process is seen to give flexibility and high quality pulp, at low production cost and high profitability.

The various process stages may be followed according to the flow diagram, Fig. 1.16.

1.6.7.1 PROCESS STAGES

1.6.7.2 DEPITHING

Claimed as the most efficient depithing technique, the wet method is used by Simon-Cusi to give an exceptionally clean fibre with minimum damage and loss. After preliminary dry screening, the loose bagasse is soaked in water at low density. It is then fed into a machine, where a high speed rotating shaft carrying many curved knives applies a vigorous scraping or peeling action to dislodge the pith from the fibre without breaking the individual fibres. Separation of pith from the fibre now takes place in a large area wet screening unit of special design. An alternative moist depithing process designed to treat the material at around 40–50% moisture content (although it produces a fibre of equal quality) gives a lower yield. The process is also less selective. Both wet and moist depithing methods may be used to treat either fresh bagasse direct from the sugar mill or material taken from store.

1.6.7.3 CHEMICAL IMPREGNATION

Maximum economy in consumption of digestion chemical is achieved by distributing the chemical liquor evenly throughout the fibrous material.

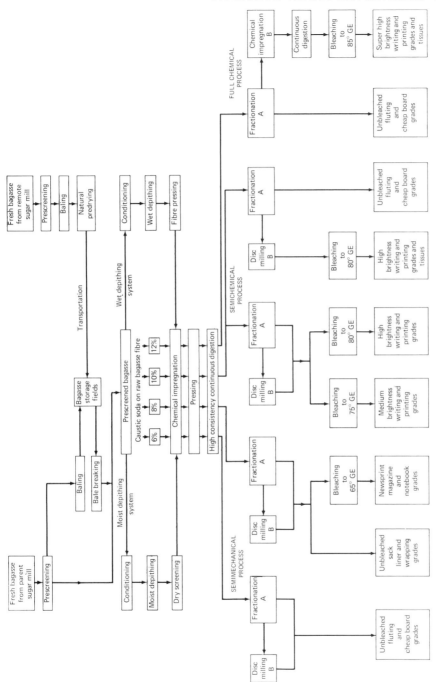

Figure 1.16 SIMON-CUSI PROCESS AS APPLIED TO BAGASSE

In this way, the softer and more chemically reactive fibre fractions do not absorb excess amounts of chemical to the detriment of the reaction with the more resistant harder fibre bundles.

The fibre must be reasonably dry to absorb the digestion chemical. Thus when wet depithing is used the fibre must first be de-watered by pressing. The digestion chemical—caustic soda and recycled strong *black liquor*—is separately heated before being metered into the depithed fibre in a specially developed impregnation tower. To ensure complete diffusion of the hot chemical into the fibre structure, the material is retained at low consistency in the tower before overflowing to a drainage conveyor feeding a continuous press. The press, of the same type as that used for de-watering wet depithed fibre, expels excess liquor which is mainly contained within the cavities of the more reactive spongy tissue. This impregnation system performs these functions: it removes water to permit absorption of chemicals; it allows sufficient time at low consistency for the chemical to soak thoroughly into all parts of the fibre; it removes surplus chemical from the reactive spongy material, at the same time forcing the chemical to penetrate further into the harder material; it provides high consistency and admits the fibre into the digester at high temperature, thus allowing an extremely rapid cooking cycle, thereby minimizing the consumption of steam for heating.

1.6.7.4 CONTINUOUS DIGESTION

Horizontal or inclined tube continuous digester units are used under vapour phase conditions. Steam is injected along the length of the tube to ensure uniform heating of the material. This initial digestion is kept short to protect the more reactive fibres from becoming degraded by overcooking.

1.6.7.5 FRACTIONATION

The pulp mass discharged from the digester is a mixture of pulp and a reactive fraction of relatively hard fibre—still consisting of large pieces of fibre or fibre bundles. These two fractions are separated by screening at low consistency. The smaller fraction, which passes through the fractionating screens, is referred to as "A" pulp. It consists almost entirely of the soft and easily pulped fibre; it also contains a trace of the parenchyma (short, thin walled cells) that has not been removed during depithing.

The larger reject fraction of partially pulped "B" fibre consists almost wholly of the larger and stronger fibres of the raw material, having a higher lignin content, a relatively low chemical activity and a high cellulose content. This "B" fibre needs further pulping. It can be done by any conventional method: it may be mechanically pulped in disc refiners to obtain a semi-chemical or semimechanical pulp, or it can be subjected to a second impregnation and digestion to give a full chemical grade of pulp with high bleachability.

1.6.7.6 SEMICHEMICAL AND SEMIMECHANICAL PULPING

At this stage, either single or two stream systems may be used: "A" and "B" pulps may either be recombined or kept separate. A single stream system is used in most cases where output is required predominantly in one grade; in this case the mixed pulps are screened and washed together.

In a two stream system the "A" and "B" pulps are screened separately. The paper produced from the "B" pulp then has higher opacity and strength. The "A" pulp can be used as a basis for certain speciality grades and is particularly suitable for a high rigidity fluting medium.

1.6.7.7 FULL CHEMICAL PULPING

When full chemical pulp is required for papers of the highest brightness a two stream system is used. The "A" and "B" pulps are screened and washed separately, and the fibrous "B" pulp undergoes a second impregnation and digestion. The second digestion is performed at higher temperature and with a higher chemical ratio than the first. This ensures that the product is effectively pulped and that it has good bleachability. Pulps produced in this way from bagasse have long fibres, high cellulose content, excellent formation properties and good tear resistance, and are comparable in every way to the best wood pulp.

1.6.8 *Peadco process*

The world's first bagasse pulping process took place in 1939 at Paramonga Mill, Peru. The process was so named for a Grace subsidiary, Process Evaluation and Development Corporation, through which it has licensed its process to several mills in various countries.

The paper/board grades currently produced at Paramonga, include: bleached writing paper (85–90% bagasse); bleached MG paper (90% bagasse); bleached tissue (75% bagasse); wrapping, multiwall sack and fluting medium (60–70% bagasse); linerboard and duplex boxboard (average 50% bagasse with purchased fibres).

In common with other bagasse pulp producing processes, the Peadco system uses depithers. In the old type, the fine or spongy pith is sucked away from the fibres—usually 1·7–1·8 mm long. New-type Peadco depithers are of the totally enclosed centrifugal separator type.

In the pulp mill are three horizontal defibrator continuous digesters. Each is 10 m long and 1 m (42 in) diameter. Caustic soda solution of 8–26% and steam of 1–1·5 lb is used per pound of bone dry pulp. Normal cooking is 15–20 min. Liquor to bone dry fibre ratio is below 2:1. Bleaching and washing equipment comprises one bleaching sequence of chlorine, caustic soda, hypochlorite sequence. Three lines of unbleached countercurrent washers, three in each line, follow. Before washing, pulp passes through three high density Claflin (wide angle) refiners. It is later screened and rejects are recycled to the digesters. The process is capable of producing 125 tons of bleached pulp per day. Pulp cleaning equipment includes 44 Bauer cleaners in two stages. The system is capable of producing pulp brightness values of 80 GE or higher with a total chlorine demand of 6%.

1.6.9 *The HF method*

This is a straw semichemical pulping process for the manufacture of fluting medium. Developed in Denmark, jointly by United Paper Mills Ltd.

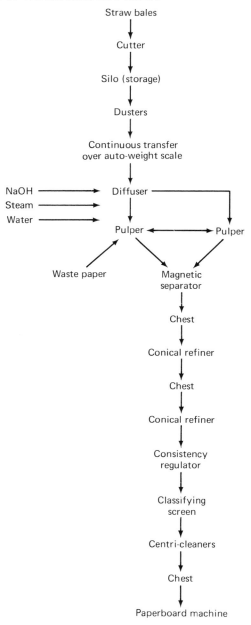

Figure 1.17. HF-METHOD FOR STRAW SEMICHEMICAL FLUTING PULP

and the Danish Sugar Corp. about 1962, it is there used to produce some 11,000 tons per year of fluting only.

The system shown in flow diagram form, Fig. 1.17, uses a patented diffuser for digesting the straw. Chopped straw is impregnated, digested and washed in a specially developed continuous flow diffusion apparatus. The HF-diffuser is a further development of the DdS-diffuser, well known in the sugar industry world.

A simple defibration and stock processing plant devised to supplement the diffuser heart of the process (Fig. 1.18) maintains the important and most desirable straw pulp fibre characteristics and properties.

1.6.9.1 OPERATION AND PRACTICE

Conventional straw cutting and dusting takes place and is followed by a special type of screw feed diffuser working on a countercurrent principle. The straw first passes through an impregnating zone, then a digesting zone and is finally continuously washed, in the last treatment zone, for the removal

Figure 1.18. HF-DIFFUSER HEART

of lignin and basically non-cellulosic plant constituents that are of little "papermaking" value.

Only a mild chemical treatment takes place to produce a high yield pulp, around 80% on the bone dry weight of straw. Cooking time is short (30 min) and at a maximum of 100°C, using caustic soda, almost 100% of which is used up during digestion. Steam consumption is exceptionally low owing to the countercurrent operation and "zone" division. Waste liquor recovery (soda recovery) is 18–20%.

The effect of continuous washing is sufficient and no further washing is needed. The pulp is removed from the diffuser by mechanical scrapers at a 12–18% consistency. Owing to the mild form of digestion, the straw still remains in "straw" form, but is easily broken down in centrifugal pulpers.

The remainder of the system is outlined in the flow diagram, Fig. 11.17, and needs no further explanation.

Fluting medium strength figures for grammages 120–130 g/m² are: burst strength, 2·5–3 kg/cm²; CMT stiffness, 25–27·2 kg (55–60 lb) for a 60% straw semichemical and 40% waste paper furnish.

1.7 refiner mechanical pulp

In effect, this is a semimechanical process, but one which relies on a pressure chemical pretreatment using about 10% by weight on material of caustic soda, soda ash or sodium sulphite in the presence of sodium carbonate or bicarbonate. The raw material (whole de-barked logs or even sawdust) is sometimes sprayed with water and chemical or treated in an autoclave, where the liquor can be forced into wood chips by pressure. Particularly suitable for pulping hardwoods, e.g., poplar (seldom bleached pulp), and continuous in operation using disc refiners, the process provides pulp mainly used as a partial substitute for conventional groundwood pulp, particularly in paperboard grades. Recovery of spent liquor is not economical. Consumption of chemical is about 1·5%. Yield is in the region of 90–92%.

The number of refiner mechanical pulp installations is growing yearly. The largest field of expansion is still in the refining of waste wood, which is available only as chips or sawdust.

1.8 thermomechanical pulping

This is one of the latest pulping techniques to come into being. Developed by Defibrator, and operated so far by one mill in Sweden, the process in its simplest terms provides for heat softening of wood chips followed by disc refining at high temperature. The pulp so produced has the feel of chemical pulp and compared to conventional groundwood pulp has a higher strength. Bulk is somewhat lower than chip groundwood pulp, but the fibre gives a higher tear and tensile strength at a given freeness. It is looked upon as an ideal replacement for conventional groundwood pulps in paperboard manufacture, especially for the "middles" and back plies, Figs. 1.19 and 1.21. In many applications it should be possible to use a much higher percentage of thermomechanical pulp than of ordinary groundwood pulp in the furnish and this is what makes the process interesting.

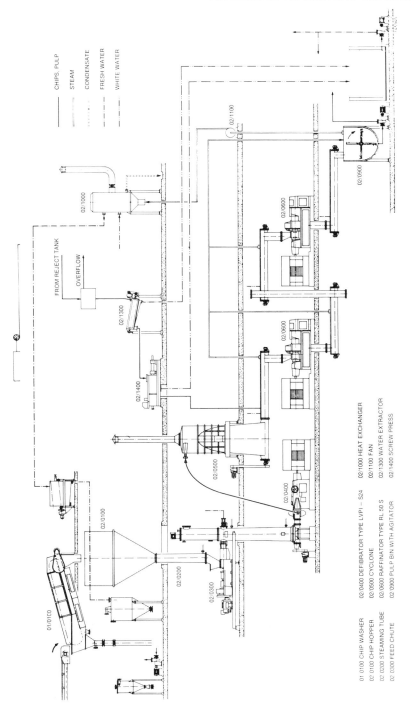

01 0100 CHIP WASHER
02 0100 CHIP HOPPER
02 0200 STEAMING TUBE
02 0300 FEED CHUTE

02/0400 DEFIBRATOR TYPE LVPI – S24
02/0500 CYCLONE
02/0600 RAFFINATOR TYPE RL 50 S
02 0900 PULP BIN WITH AGITATOR

02/1000 HEAT EXCHANGER
02/1100 FAN
02/1300 WATER EXTRACTOR
02/1400 SCREW PRESS

Figure 1.19. THERMOMECHANICAL PULP PROCESS

CHIPS, PULP
STEAM
CONDENSATE
FRESH WATER
WHITE WATER

FROM REJECT TANK

OVERFLOW

Figure 1.20.   THERMOMECHANICAL PULP DIGESTER
In the Asplund Defibrator thermomechanical pulping process, chips drop from the base of a presteaming vessel, to a screw feeder and then pass into a vertical digesting vessel (pre-heater) under 140 °C at 3 atmos., pressure. Seen here is the base of the digesting vessel from which the de-fibrated chips are screw-fed into a 42 in single-disc defibrator unit rotating at 1,500 rpm (at right).

1.9 the rôle of birch pulp in paperboards

1.9.1 *The birch fibre*

In recognizing that fibre form and the surface structure of fibres are both influential in the development of stress/strain characteristics in paper and paperboard, it is difficult to describe the dimensional characteristics of different fibres in simple terms. Fibre length and fibre width are less important in papermaking technology today than they ever have been. Short fibred pulps are becoming increasingly important—not only those of hardwoods, but from other raw materials, e.g., straw, bagasse, bamboo, etc. The most important information concerning short fibres is fibre wall thickness, hence fibre stiffness; and its shape. Is it ribbon-like or rod-like, etc? Typical of short fibres is that they are not only short, but also are thin (see Fig. 1.12). The term, "short fibres" is therefore not descriptive today. These fibres favour good formation, Fig. 1.21 (a)(b). Their slenderness in particular increases sheet surface smoothness.

Birch fibres fall about midway in comparison with the typical ribbon-like fibres of aspen and the rod-like fibres of beech and oak. All are hardwoods.

1.9.1.1 SINGLE FIBRE STRENGTH

The strength properties of single fibres have become of increased importance lately. Figures for hardwoods and softwoods differ. Interesting figures

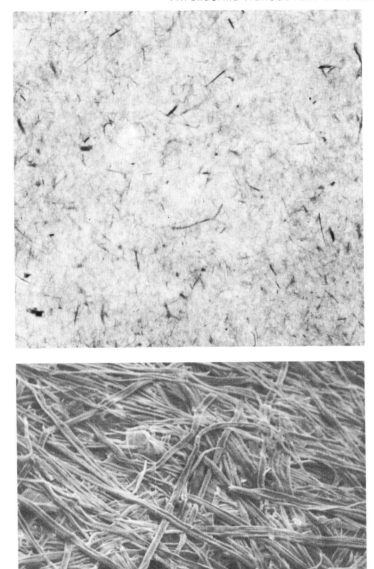

Figure 1.21 (a) and (b).   FIBRES OF BIRCH FAVOUR GOOD FORMATION
             (b).   Surface of 90% birch fibre sheet.

have been recorded on elongation at rupture. A figure of 6·2% strain at failure has been recorded for birch sulphate compared with a 4·2% for spruce sulphite. A difference in elongation also appears when comparing stress/strain curves of papers prepared from different types of fibres. Other conditions remaining equal, coarser pine fibres, for example, need to be beaten more compared with the thinner fibres of aspen in order to achieve the same tensile strength. Young's modulus for extensional stiffness is higher for pine and, at the same time, elongation at rupture is higher for the aspen sheet. Explanation for this is difficult at the present time. It could be due to low tensile strength of the softwood fibres or high elongation of the hardwood fibres. Most important perhaps, it could also be owing just to a more even and continuous redistribution of stresses during loading in the case of aspen paper, which is built up of a very large number of fibres, compared with pine pulp sheets. Anyhow, such behaviour appears of considerable importance in strength property comparisons of paper/board when formed of fibres with different dimensions and different single fibre strength properties. Naturally, high extensional stiffness involves the use of more fibrous material to carry the load achieved through more bonding. It has been already suggested that in concept the term "formation pulps" better expresses the most important papermaking properties of hardwood fibres.

1.9.1.2 SHORT FIBRES MEANS "GOOD FORMATION"

It is likewise no easier to make a simple comparison of the "paper-making" properties of a pulp of varying fibre dimensions. Coarseness, fibre length and the number of fibres making up a sheet of given basis weight varies widely for different pulps, Fig. 1.22(a)(b)(c)(d). The number of fibres in a given area influence the bonded network structure. It also influences the way redistribution of stresses and strains in the sheet will take place during loading and elongation. This is a particularly significant observation in the case of fluting mediums—see section 7.9.4.

It can generally be stated that coarse fibres (Fig. 1.23) form bulky sheets with few bonds, high opacity, high tear and low tensile strength. Long fibres distribute a local stress concentration over a greater area. In this way, wet web strength and tear strength are increased by long fibres—cross refer section 7.9.5.

These disparities are in many cases reflected in the practice of beating the long fibred pulp component (in a mixed furnish) first of all in order to improve formation and surface smoothness.

Modern short fibre pulps are relatively strong. They can be used separately or in a mixture with longer fibre pulps in the manufacture of many paper/board grades. Important about short fibres is that not only are they strong enough to substitute long fibre pulps, e.g., as again in the case of fluting mediums, but they do possess certain unique properties. This places them in a class of their own regarding formation and surface smoothness. Short fibres usually mean good formation. Thin fibres mean a smooth paper surface. The influence on structure and smoothness is clearly seen in Figs. 7.37(a)–7.41.

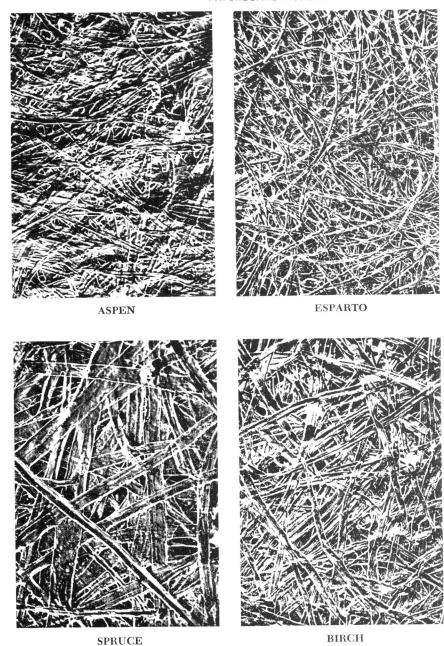

ASPEN

ESPARTO

SPRUCE

BIRCH

Figures 1.22 (a). (b). (c) and (d). FIBRE COARSENESS LENGTH AND NUMBER IN THE SHEET VARIES WIDELY FOR DIFFERENT PULPS

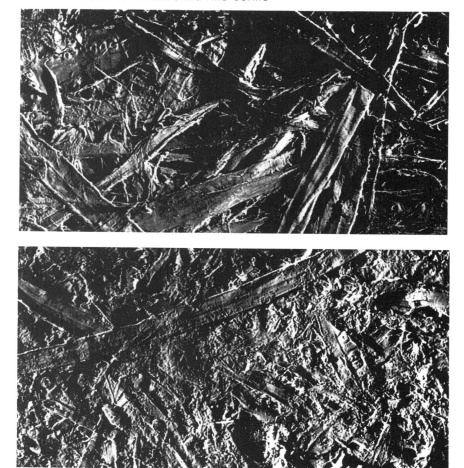

Figure 1.23. COARSE FIBRES FORM BULKY SHEETS

I.IO NSSC **birch pulp for fluting**

The birch tree grows in prolific abundance in forests of the Northern hemisphere. Hitherto it has found relatively little outlet as a papermaking pulp. But in the last few years it has been discovered to be of great value as the major pulp component in the manufacture of fluting medium for corrugating.

Birch, of which there are many species and families, has fibres typical of other hardwoods. Shorter than softwoods, they are still relatively long but thicker. They are somewhat easily fibrilated during beating to give a bulky and stiff sheet.

Fluting medium made from semichemically processed birch fibres, it has been claimed, exhibits the following properties: except for bursting strength, all properties of the corrugated board and box are improved—flat crush, edge crush, box compression resistance, puncture resistance and shock absorbing performance. Practical running conditions on the corrugator, are claimed as also improved. But in the light of runnability trials it appears that the presence of a proportion of long fibres in the furnish is necessary to achieve optimum corrugator performance—see section 7.9.5 and conclusion.

Under today's raw materials economic situation, optimal board construction is obtained when using raw materials that feature the lowest price per unit crush resistance. Currently, semichemical birch fluting pulp (high yield), ranks economically most desirable. In fact, at equal basis weight it has 15–20% higher crush resistance than kraft liner and is more than 100% higher than many waste based fluting grades. The economic consequences of this are clearly obvious.

As a general comment, it is both significant and interesting to note, that in a series of comparisons made in refining short and long fibred pulp, both together and separately, there was no noticeably distinct difference. The fibres of the short fibred pulp were shortened less when refined together than when refined as a separate fibre component. With the long fibred pulp, quite the contrary applies. On the whole, the shortening of birch fibre, especially birch sulphate fibre, during refining is quite insignificant, provided refining is not prolonged. Within practical papermaking bounds, it is generally unnecessary and certainly undesirable to cause fibre shortening of birch pulp through prolonged refining, in the manufacture of the majority of today's papers and paperboards. When making paper grades, birch pulp also is able to impart improvement to a number of properties such as: opacity, smoothness, formation, etc.

1.11 birch pulp in kraft linerboard

It is probably still not so generally well known that, within 30% additions, unbleached birch sulphate pulp can be added in the surface layer of kraft linerboard without materially influencing important strength properties. Tearing strength and folding endurance are known to be impaired at fibre additions exceeding this amount. However, surface properties, e.g., peeling resistance, have been shown to be substantially improved, as also to some extent has printing smoothness.

1.12 birch pulp in folding carton board

Special food board in particular is made from bleached sulphate pulp. It has been established that several of the properties of this board may be improved if a part of the basic pulp component (bleached pine sulphate) is replaced by bleached birch sulphate. The addition of birch at around 30% has been found to increase tensile strength and stretch of the board. It somewhat reduces the folding endurance ability and of the board to crease. In this latter respect, however, its undesirable influence appears important only when large additions of the birch pulp component are made.

In general, the addition of birch pulp reduces the bulk and porosity and the paraffin absorption of the board. These effects are however, greatly dependent upon the "beating speed" of the birch pulp components—and equally upon the beating equipment. The extent of beating in the manufacture of this type of board favours fibrillation of the fibres only, with the minimum amount of cutting.

Bleached birch sulphate and sulphite pulp are commonly used in the surface layer of folding boxboard grades. Apart from folding endurance, other strength properties are not affected by the addition of birch fibres to the basic softwood pulp component.

Maximum limits to the addition of birch pulp in a furnish may be determined both by the acceptable limit of its effect on folding endurance and by a measure of its tendency towards a decrease in surface strength, and increased fluffing. The latter rises with the amount of birch fibre added. According to information, the addition of birch pulp may be satisfactorily made up to an amount of 50% or more. It clearly improves formation of the surface layer and results in greater sheet opacity.

1.13 pulp production techniques for fluting medium

1.13.1 *Swedish mill practice*

An interesting semichemical pulp mill for fluting manufacture belongs to a Swedish firm. The company, in 1968, were the first to use a Kamyr digester for NSSC pulping. This also features an inclined top separator for pre-impregnation.

According to Fig. 1.24 chips are metered through a low pressure feeder into a horizontal steaming vessel and retained for 2·5 min at a pressure of 1·2 kg/cm². The pre-steamed chips fall via a chip chute into a high pressure feeder, and are then transported by liquor circulation to the inclined top separator. This cooking liquor is added by a high pressure pump so that impregnation takes place in the pipeline leading to the separator and in the bottom of this unit. The chips are screwed upwards into the top of the digester while the circulating liquor is drawn off at the bottom.

Some cooking liquor is added at the top of the digester, which is rapidly heated along with the chips by a direct steam flow added at the top of the column. NaOH consumption is about 85 kg per ton of wood, and the ratio of wood-to-liquor is 2:1.

Although the initial cooking conditions involved a vapour stage at the top of the digester, in practice cooking is in the liquor phase with the pile of chips rising slightly above the liquor level. Pressure in the digester is 8·5–9 kg/cm². An air compressor was installed but has not been required since this pressure level can be attained by steam injection alone.

The chip level is measured by a gamma ray detector and controlled by the rate of withdrawal of cooked chips out of the bottom of the column. The liquor level is controlled by the addition of wash liquor at the bottom.

The chips are cooked for about one hour at 172°C and then washed for three hours at 125°C by countercurrent treatment in the diffusion washing zone. Under these conditions, yield is 84%. The countercurrent flow is achieved by extracting liquor from the strainers at the top of the washing zone.

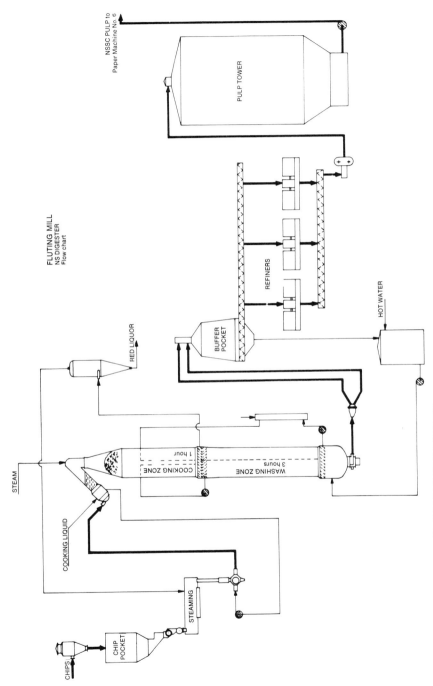

Figure 1.24. FLUTING MILL PULP PREPARATION FLOWCHART

There was some question about the efficiency of diffusion washing for the NSSC pulp which was expected to block the diffusional paths due to its almost unchanged structure. However, in practice the results were excellent. In the three hour washing time about 85% of the solids in the waste liquor are recovered, at a dilution factor of 1·5.

For maximum strength characteristics, the chips are cooled to about 90°C before blowing to a buffer bin. This unit has a strainer bottom for the liquor to flow off and results in chips at 25% dryness.

A screw conveyor bin feeds the chips to a battery of three Sund-Bauer 412 disc refiners operating in parallel, each of 1,500 hp. Water is added to flush the chips into the refiners and also to bring consistency down to about 20% dryness. The refiners consume 105 kWh/ton of 90% pulp giving a freeness of 16–19°SR.

The defibrated stock is conveyed to a high density storage tank and then via a dilution tank to a battery of three Sund-Bauer 441 disc refiners. The refiners operate on a triple coupling system with one unit for kraft pulp, the middle one used as spare, and the third for the NSSC pulp. The refiners here consume about 30 kWh/ton producing pulp with a freeness of 24–26°SR. The semichemical and kraft pulps are blended in a chest and then sent to two Selectifier screens for cleaning before the headbox.

The brown liquor recovered from the in-digester washing is returned to the kraft pulp mill to be added to the kraft chemical recovery system permitting so-called cross recovery. In this system the NSSC liquor is used to make up for the losses in the kraft recovery cycle. Normally one requires three times as much kraft pulp output as NSSC in order to strike the necessary balance.

1.13.2 *Finnish mill practice*

One of the largest fluting mills in Europe is in Finland. Here the company currently operates a single paperboard machine of capacity 150,000 tons/year of fluting in the range 80–220 g/m². The machine has a trim width of 6·5 m and a maximum speed of 700 m/min (2,350 ft/min).

The pulping operation comprises a 465 m-ton/day continuous Defibrator digester.

NSSC cooking is carried out using an ammonium based liquor. At the present time, this is reportedly the world's largest digester unit of its type in continuous operation.

In the mill, birch logs are chipped and blown by a pneumatic conveyor to a chip washer. The washed chips enter a pre-steaming vessel and are then conveyed into a 40 cm diameter (16 in) screw feeder. This feeds the chips into an impregnating vessel containing the cooking liquor at digester steam pressure, equal to 8–10 kg/cm². The impregnating vessel is of a new design with one, single, large, horizontal screw located at the bottom for transporting the chips upwards through the cooking liquor. This procedure assures complete liquor penetration and impregnation of the chips. The chips are allowed to expand, thereby absorbing the cooking liquor. Retention time in the impregnating vessel is 7–13 min.

From the top of the impregnating vessel a horizontal screw transfers the impregnated chips to the vertical digester where a 20 min cook is completed in vapour phase. The chips move continuously downwards by gravity through the digester and are discharged by a flow valve through a cyclone.

From the cyclone the diluted pulpy mass (about 18% concentration) is conveyed to three 106 cm (42 in) disc refiners. Here, defibration takes place under atmospheric pressure. The pulp is now washed on pressure filters and recovered waste liquor is pumped to the evaporater and burned. Washed pulp is finally refined in two further discs at about 5% consistency.

1.13.3 *Dutch mill practice*

In contrast to the Swedish and Finnish method for producing semi-chemical pulp for fluting medium earlier described is the process operated by one of Holland's leading corrugated board producers.

Here, hardwoods of all species are used, gathered from all over Holland. They include birch, poplar, oak and some fruit trees. Unbarked and un-selected logs pass directly to two chippers (145 cm diameter and 190 cm diameter six knife unit). Chips are then conveyed through a vibrating screen and metered into a screw feeder delivering to the inlet chamber of a 65 ton/day Pandia digester. Of importance to note is that the entire pulp plant is handled by one operator and an assistant.

Chips are cooked for about 21 min at 12·6 kg/cm² (180 lb/in²) and a temperature of 170°C in a liquor of sodium sulphite and sodium carbonate. Consumption of chemical is about 10% and 4% respectively. After conveying to a blow tank, the pulp is diluted to 12% consistency and is passed through an 81 cm (36 in) hydrodisc refiner. Washing of the pulp follows over a self-priming filter. Liquor from the filter is used for spot dilution before the first refining and washing. This takes place in a second 81 cm hydrodisc refiner. After consistency control, the stock receives a final refining treatment in a single disc refiner and is then metered to the paper machine chest. Here it is mixed with waste paper stock.

This mill uses unselected waste paper which is treated in a 6 m (20 ft) diameter, 250 tons/day Hydrapulper equipped with Vokes rotor and flote purge system (see section 1.16.**1**). Conventional waste paper stock preparation processing takes place—sections 1.15/1.16/1.17.

1.13.4 *Japanese mill practice*

An interesting NSSC mill in Japan, large producers of fluting medium and linerboard, uses duplicate preparation systems to produce 300 tons of pulp per day for fluting medium. The raw materials for the mill are northern-type hardwoods, e.g., alder, birch, maple, elm, oak, willow, etc. These are in abundant supply but vary widely in specific gravity according to species. Because of this, the mill is split into two independent, parallel production systems each of 150 ton capacity. Light weight hardwoods are handled in one line and heavy hardwoods in the other—an interesting solution to the problem of a uniform, high quality production in spite of wide raw material variations.

A notable feature is the omission of all barking equipment from the system. Unbarked wood is chipped and screened in the usual manner. With the use of an efficient cleaning system, cooking bark with the wood results in a 3–6% increase in pulp yield, without sacrifice in product quality.

Chips are metered to a digester pre-heater. Here they are steamed with digester exhaust steam. Cooking takes place in a stainless steel digester, 152 cm (5 ft) in diameter by 4 m (55 ft) long. The yield of NSSC pulp is approximately 80%.

Cooked chips are discharged into a live bottom blow bin. From here they pass through disc refiners for high density liquor extraction.

The mill is unusual for an NSSC plant, in that it is equipped with its own liquor system. This is completely independent of the kraft recovery system, except for liquor burning. This feature together with a separate NSSC black liquor evaporation plant, allows a 1 : 1 ratio of NSSC to kraft tonnage, without upsetting the chemical balance in either system. Normal cooking conditions are a time of 20 min, at 180°C in a liquor consisting of 16% sodium sulphite (Na_2SO_3) and 25% sodium carbonate (Na_2CO_3) on oven dry weight of wood.

Interesting to note, in passing, is that this mill belonging to Honshu Paper Manufacturing Company, is the first mill to succeed in making liner-board using hardwood kraft pulp. The operation began in 1959 and is regarded as a unique accomplishment in the papermaking world.

secondary fibre materials

1.14 waste paper processing and principles

Despite difficulties caused by contaminants, waste paper (*paperstock*) remains an increasingly important economic source of secondary fibres for board-making (and more and more for paper making), particularly in countries where most virgin pulp supplies have to be imported.

In Europe and in North America and to an increasing extent in other countries, regenerated de-inked waste paper is largely being used as a general replacement for groundwood. This is especially the case in paperboard manufacture, where a number of the pulp requirements for the "middles" and back liners of multi-ply boards can be satisfactorily substituted by de-inked waste. Moreover, the use of de-inked waste is known to have the capability of improving sheet formation and drainage on the forming wire. Its use as a fibre component in some packaging papers and boards (particularly in the manufacture of fluting medium) is believed to contribute certain physical characteristics felt to be of particular practical importance in converting operations. This is probably due largely to the thermochemical treatment to which waste paper is subjected during regeneration—particularly the ground-wood containing lignin component.

In waste paper processing it is essential to choose equipment and processes which minimize fibre shrinkage and cause as little damage to the fibres as possible. Only slushing or de-fibring with a minimum amount of cutting is needed, as fibres in waste paper have already been pre-treated.

Some European continental mills still apparently prefer recovery systems using conventional-type breakers with perforated back fall and kollergangs.

But, modern systems involve centrifugal disintegrating equipment, such as continuously running, modified Hydrapulpers and appropriate accessory cleaning equipment. Slushing without heat application insures maximum retention of fines, sizing agents, etc., but is only suitable for certain types of sorted waste. In most other cases it is necessary to use alkalis and other digestion aids and to cook at high temperatures (45°–80°C).

Equipment used in de-inking is basically the same as for general waste paper de-fibring and cooking. Opinion varies as to whether de-inking should precede cooking. But whatever the procedure, ink should be made into a stable dispersion as soon as it is separated from the fibres, in order to obtain effective de-inking and to prevent agglomerated ink particles from re-depositing on the fibres. The process is assisted by the presence of chemicals during pulping. Generally, increasing the temperature reduces the cooking cycle, probably because heat tends to soften ink and other non-fibrous materials, thereby increasing the effectiveness of chemical action and of dispersion by means of abrasion and shearing action. High temperatures also favour rapid de-fibring except with groundwood papers which de-fibre and de-ink better at lower temperatures, e.g., 38–71°C against 71–99°C for low groundwood content papers. De-fibring and de-inking are often more effective at higher consistencies—high density cooking may approach 40%.

Choice of de-inking chemicals depends on the type of waste paper being treated, but caustic soda and soda ash (sodium carbonate) are commonly used alkalis, either singly or in combination. Alkaline reagents, in particular sodium silicate, aid de-fibring; breakdown of the printing ink vehicle; saponification of neutral resins and sizing agents; neutralization of alum and detachment of coatings of ink from fibres. Up to 3% sodium silicate in the presence of caustic soda and soda ash will reduce discoloration of ground-wood in mixed papers and promote better cleanliness. Use of sodium and hydrogen peroxide with alkali are also finding increasing favour, especially for high groundwood content papers, and may be used with sodium silicate in concentrations up to 5–6%. Zinc hydrosulphite is also used as an aid to colour removal with high groundwood content papers (section 13.6).

Sodium peroxide has the double advantage of providing the alkalinity necessary to saponify the ink vehicle (thus making extra alkali unnecessary) and of possessing an oxidizing action that helps to prevent the yellowing of the pulp by the combined action of alkalinity and elevated temperatures. It should not be necessary to use more than 2%, based on the weight of dry cellulose material.

Sodium silicate has the advantage, besides its alkalinity, of preventing the redeposition of ink pigment particles on the pulp and should be employed as a 4% solution of density 36°Bé, based on the dry weight of material.

The concentration of cellulose material should not exceed 8% in the treating solution, otherwise penetration is impeded and, although variations in pH value appear not to have much influence on the whiteness of the final pulp, it has been found advantageous to adjust the reaction of the solution to the range pH 11–11·5 for newsprint and pH 10·5–11 for art papers.

Other de-inking aids comprise fillers, such as *bentonite*, which acts as an ink particle suspending aid, i.e., its function is to prevent the removed pigments from being redeposited on the fibres; and chemicals such as hydrocarbon oils, alkali phosphates and ammonia.

1.14.1 *De-inking methods*

Two types of process are available for the removal of ink particles once these are separated from the fibres. They are ink removal by *washing* and ink removal by *flotation*. The latter process is most favoured.

Ink removal by washing traditionally takes place by repeated de-watering and dilution of the stock, on the same type of machines that are used in treating pulps.

1.14.2 *Flotation de-inking*

To render waste paper stock suitable for flotation de-inking, necessary chemicals are added to the pulper during slushing (about 30 min) either at a normal temperature or near 45–48°C according to whether it is ground-wood or wood-free at a 5–7% BD (bone dry) fibre consistency. Low ("cold") temperature slushing needs a longer dissolving time. After slushing, stock is dumped into a chest, where soaking takes place for about $1\frac{1}{2}$–2 hours. Light contraries are rejected by a high consistency purifier. Subsequently, the pulp is "de-specked" in a de-flaker—section 2.2.1. Pulp is then diluted to a consistency of about 0.8% BD fibre and the diluted stock flotated, when printing ink particles are removed in the flotation cells. The accepted stock coming from the primary flotation stage is now thickened to a 4–6% BD consistency, and is ready for usual paper mill preparation.

Flotation rejects may account for 5–10% by weight of raw material according to waste paper grade and fillers content.

For de-inking of groundwood content waste grades, usually done in the cold, about 3–5% sodium silicate with 2% sodium peroxide and 3.5% soft soap, with a fatty acid content of about 42%, is commonly added to the pulper. The action of the alkali is mainly to detach ink particles ready for removal during flotation.

The sodium silicate is used mainly as a stabilizer for peroxide; it also has the properties of wetting, saponification of oily inks, dispersion of pigments, suspension of ink and dirt and protects fibres from re-absorption of loosened soil. Silicates lift ink from fibre surfaces, they do not dissolve it. Unlike stronger alkalis, silicates do not yellow groundwood stock. This is important and is due to de-inking being carried out at a lower pH than with normal alkalis.

Caustic soda is not needed if sodium peroxide is used, as the latter produces caustic soda in the reaction:

$$Na_2O_2 + H_2O \rightarrow 2NaOH + O_2$$

In parallel with the action of de-inking, the peroxide also serves as a bleaching agent by the liberation of oxygen, while the soap partly acts as a washing and dispersing agent along with the silicate. The principal application of the soap, however, is as the flotation agent, at which stage, its inherent soap properties—the formation of insoluble calcium soaps in conjunction with the calcium ions of water—are utilized. These calcium soaps create sticky flakes, on which the detached printing ink particles and dispersed air bubbles collect, and float to the surface ready for scum removal as froth. Conditions of flow velocities are controlled so that released fibres are separately washed away and conserved.

Equally satisfactory de-inking results can be achieved by initial pre-impregnation of the waste with the required chemicals at a consistency around 30%. By this means slushing time in the pulper is shortened and takes place at normal temperature, and the process is continuous.

For de-inking of woodfree waste, usually 3–5% caustic soda is used in the pulper at a temperature of 60–80 °C. For de-inking woodfree coloured waste, bleaching can take place in a chest by soaking using sodium hydrosulphite. An improvement in whiteness may be obtained by hypochlorite bleaching after flotation.

The accompanying Fig. 1.25 is a schematic layout for a de-inking system using both groundwood and woodfree waste paper in a paperboard mill manufacturing bleached top liner. In such a system of 20–22 tons/day of pulp, by careful selection of waste paper grade, a bleached pulp brightness as high as 73–83% Zeiss-Elrepho can be achieved.

1.14.2.1 DE-INKING SYSTEM OPERATIONAL DETAILS

As Fig. 1.25 is a "closed water" system, only *back water* from the thickener is used in the pulper, where consistency is about 6%. In woodfree de-inking the water temperature is raised to 55–60 °C, using live steam in the pulper. The requisite chemicals are now added after a short initial mixing, the pulper being operated on a continuous basis. The pulper dump chest(s) should be large enough to permit about one hour's retention time. Coarse cleaning follows to remove small light contraries, e.g., paper clips, rubber bands, etc., from whence stock is passed to a battery of de-flakers to reduce flakes and fibre bundles. After adjusting consistency to 1% ahead of a vibrating screen and partly in the mixing cells, the flotation process begins in its primary stages.

In the flotation cells, finely dispersed air and chemicals cause printing ink particles to flock together in the individual cells and float to the surface, where as a foam scum they are separated out. The separated fibre stock is now cleaned on a fine slotted enclosed screen (to remove plastics, etc.), in classifiers and washed on rotary filters and is then gradually thickened to about 40% consistency in disc presses.

The thickened pulp is now sent to a single shaft de-fibring unit and at the same time bleaching liquor is added. The pulp, according to traditional bleaching practice with rags, is allowed to remain in storage silos for about 8–10 days. Here continuous slow bleaching will take place, after which the pulp is finally washed and ready for use.

DISC PRESS. A disc press consists of two vertically mounted rotating discs, with screen plates on the same shaft, inclined at an angle to each other. The

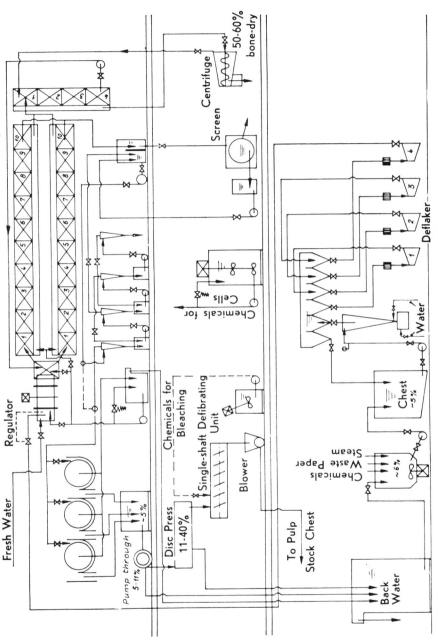

Figure 1.25.   DE-INKING SYSTEM FOR GROUNDWOOD AND WOODFREE WASTE PAPER TREATMENT

stock enters between the discs at the point of greatest separation and is carried round by rotation to the closest gap, where the increased pressure forces the water out through the holes of the screen plates. The stock must be between 10–12% concentration before it can be passed to the disc press.

1.14.3 *Separation of printing ink*

Printing ink more or less consists of a pigment, a binder and various additives. Some inks are easier to remove from the surface of cellulose fibres than are others. Alkaline chemicals prove the most suitable practical means of achieving their removal from waste paper. The removal mechanism works thus: the binder becomes softened by the alkali in combination with heat or mechanical agitation and soaking and looses its pigment binding power— the pigment becomes separated from the fibres—and, providing it is not re-attracted to the fibres' surface, it can be induced to float off using known principles.

Unfortunately, not all inks react in the same way towards alkali owing to a widely differing nature in their respective binders. Table 1.3 indicates known printing ink binders and their reactivity.

Table 1.3.   PRINTING INK BINDERS

Easy to remove	*Hard to remove*
Natural rosin	Asphalt
Modified rosin	Cellulose derivates
Cumaron	Synthetic latices
Turpentine rosin	Phenol urea resins
Petroleum rosin	Melamine resins
Alkyd resin	
Drying oil	

1.14.4 *pH importance in de-inking*

Groundwood—After the ink particles have been torn away from the surface of the fibres by a de-flaking action, pH becomes increasingly important. In practice it is necessary to maintain a pH 6·5–7·0 at the de-flaking stage. If it swings away from the neutral point (7·0), the surface tension of the process is altered and then the flotation system will not function properly.

It is especially difficult to remove inks and dirt in the flotation cells if the pH is below 6·0–7·5, since the important and necessary foam development is either accelerated or retarded. A change in pH counteracts the foaming agents, very quickly changes the surface tension and disturbs the flotation operation.

Woodfree—The de-inking of woodfree papers requires stronger chemical concentrations in the pulper. This is because of the usually harder and better type of printing inks used on woodfree papers. It is for this reason also that the working temperature is higher. This accelerates the chemical activity. At the same time it improves the detergent action of the pulper chemicals. After the required reaction time the process is neutralized with a weak acid and then adjusted to about pH 6·7. De-flaking follows.

The pH neutralization and adjustment is most important. If the pH drops below pH 5·5, redisposition of printing ink particles onto the fibres (some of which show a strong affinity) will occur. If it occurs the resultant "blackness" cannot be removed, even during the strong attrition action in the de-flakers.

POWER CONSUMPTION. The total power consumption for a de-inking layout as described earlier for groundwood waste paper would be around 49 kWh/100 kg, and for woodfree waste paper about 71 kWh/100 kg (kilowatt hours per 100 kg of de-inked material).

1.15 waste paper processing equipment

A modern Hydrapulper operating on a continuous basis is shown in Fig. 1.26. The design is basically the same as for Hydrapulpers used in batch unit operation, but certain refinements are included. These consist of the use of a *ragger rope* and a *junk remover*.

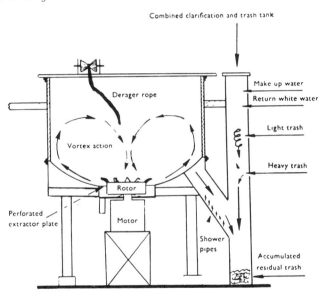

Figure 1.26.   HYDRAPULPER FOR CONTINUOUS SLUSHING OF WASTE PAPER

Ragger rope—This is a thick rope that dangles in the pulper vortex and "collects" waste in the form of rags, string, wire, etc. The rope is cut into disposable lengths and removed. To start the deragging action, wire is wrapped round the rope.

Junk remover—This commonly consists of a vertical bucket elevator, connected to the base of the pulper, through which "junk" passes. Heavy material settles at the base of the box, and it is removed by rising buckets. Lighter materials float on the surface and are collected on the upward passage of the buckets. To permit the efficient removal of junk, extraction base plates in the pulper tub are perforated with holes at least 1·9–3·1 cm diameter, through which fibre stock can continually pass.

Advanced techniques using specialized equipment as indicated in the accompanying flow diagrams enable the separation of *pernicious* contraries of nearly all types found in mixed waste.

Purge system—A relatively recent development of importance has been the flote purge system used in the removal of non-fibrous constituents of waste papers, e.g., synthetic-type packaging films of low specific gravity. These materials float on the surface of the stock being slushed in the pulper and present trash removal difficulties. Mechanical handling equipment is not readily suited to its removal. The flote purge system is a self-purging module connected to the pulper tub through a slot about 31 cm below operating level. It continuously and automatically removes floating rejects during slushing. The slot is kept clear by a continuously rotating scraper arm. Rejects are fed to a Drubber—a totally enclosed machine, fitted with a series of rotors designed to produce violent turbulent action, which scrubs fibres free from adhering foreign matter. A special pump delivers 0·5% consistency stock to a slow running enclosed conical screen. Screen "accepts" are returned to the system. It is important to note that the average dry solids content of received waste paper is 90%. The average from a modern system is about 92–94% solids on OD weight of material.

1.16 accessory de-fibring equipment

The need for improved techniques in the disintegrating of wet stock has led to the introduction of new equipment and improvements to existing machines.

Modern paper technology requires that a distinction is made between the mechanical actions involved in "breaking" or slushing, and the further actions of de-fibring that more generally occur in the initial stages of beating/refining.

Before the introduction of centrifugal disintegrating equipment like the Hydrapulper, the breaker or breaker/beater was largely used to reduce pulp, dry mill broke and waste paper into slush. This was slow and expensive and consequently led to a development in improved slushing methods. However, the process of slushing merely accomplishes an initial reduction in "particle" size of the fibrous material. This takes place relatively quickly, but, depending on the equipment, still leaves the stuff largely in the form of fibre bundles and large pulp flakes. Because it is costly, inefficient and unsatisfactory to run the pulper past this point in an effort to achieve further de-fibration (which only takes place increasingly slowly) it was and is still fairly common practice to pass stuff in this incompletely de-fibrated state through high speed refiners. Sometimes refiners are run in a "backed-off" position to achieve de-fibration in the initial pass, for later recycling and refining in further passes; alternatively such initial measure is dispensed with. In either instance it is costly and inefficient to run refiners in this manner. In itself this aggravates stock heterogeneity, as a proportion of the stuff invariably receives harsher treatment.

In consequence two solutions proved practical. One of these took the form of the successful development of an improved centrifugal pulper rotor plus bedplate. The other was the introduction of a completely separate de-fibring machine to effect proper disintegration of fibre bundles and flakes after slushing. These de-fibring machines are known as de-flakers or fiberizers.

1.16.1 *Hydrapulper Vokes rotor*

Efforts to improve slushing efficiency of conventional Hydrapulpers led a few years ago to the introduction of the Vokes rotor. In principle, this consists of eight hydrafoil-shaped vanes, rotating above a stationary bedplate. The bedplate (*attrition ring*) consists of a series of chrome-steel heat-treated bars interspersed by grooves. Provision for built-in adjustment of rotor-to-bedplate clearance is made. The Vokes rotor, used in conjunction with a perforated bedplate, Fig. 1.27, permits continuous stuff extraction from the pulper. Close proximity of the rotating vanes keeps the extraction holes clear of unde-fibred flakes.

Figure 1.27. VOKES ROTOR WITH EXTENDED BEDPLATE

On batch operation a Vokes rotor Hydrapulper is capable of 100% de-fibring, and at equal horsepower can provide 60% more de-fibring than with a conventional Hydrapulper rotor. With the "new" type rotor it is possible to achieve an output of 162 tons per day with a 4·2 m (14 ft) dia. batch pulper slushing bleached kraft—an increase of 100 tons over the conventional rotor (no bedplate).

The Vokes rotor enables pulpers to be used to treat: all pulps, "mixed" waste paper including grades difficult to pulp, such as wet strength, etc.

1.16.2 *De-flakers or fiberizers*

In a short time these special purpose machines have become almost indispensable in modern papermaking practice. There are several types of which the Escher Wyss de-flaker, Fig. 1.28; the Scott–Rietz durafiner, Fig. 1.29; and the Bolton–Emerson de-flaker are typical. In accordance with the originally intended purpose, these machines effect the reduction of flakes in fibre stock suspensions into individual fibre components without damage to fibre structure. The Scott–Rietz durafiner and Bolton–Emerson de-flaker, are both vertical units and therefore also accomplish screening.

Other uses to which de-flakers are put include hot-stock screening in the pulp industry. In this process, pulp is conveyed directly from the blow pit following digestion, via de-flakers to closed rotary screens. The reject is conveyed either to the digesters or returned to the blow pit. Fibre knots and shive circulate until mechanical treatment or chemical action has loosened their fibre components. The pulp is not washed until such de-fibration and screening are completed. Hot waste liquors are drained from the washing tanks and evaporated. In this relatively new pulping technique (see section 12.3.1.6), the de-flaker can be used with advantage as a de-fibrator.

The de-flaker, in pulp manufacture, is also used for: treating rejects, either before or after screening, for "bast" and bark particles remaining after centrifugal cleaning and de-fibration of annual plants like straw and bagasse.

The method of operation is a combined action of mechanical impact forces, hydrodynamic shear stresses, fibre-to-fibre friction and pressure pulsations. The effect on fibres was originally erroneously attributed to ultrasonic effects, which are known to modify fibre structure satisfactorily, but as yet cannot be harnessed in practice.

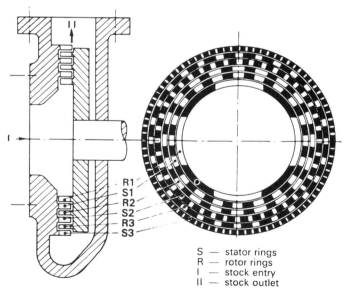

R1
S1
R2
S2
R3
S3

S — stator rings
R — rotor rings
I — stock entry
II — stock outlet

Figure 1.28. ELEMENTS OF THE ESCHER WYSS DEFLAKER

1.16.2.1 ESCHER WYSS DE-FLAKER (Fig. 1.28)

All working parts are enclosed in a horizontal pump-type housing and consist of a number of teeth separated by slots, arranged on concentric rotor and stator rings spaced 1 mm apart. The number of teeth increases from the inside outwards, while the slots decrease in size.

As stuff enters (as shown), the rotor teeth R1 drive the fibres centrifugally against the teeth on the stator ring S1, thenceforth through the other rotor and stator rings, until exit takes places in a radial direction at S3.

This machine will handle: newsprint, "mixed" waste paper, coated paper, strawpulp, glassine, etc. Average operating conditions are:

Newsprint: 5% consistency; throughput 45 tons/day, 1 pass
"Mixed" waste: 4·5% consistency; throughput 42 tons/day, 1 pass
Coated paper (coating dispersion): 2·5% consistency; throughput 20 tons/day, 3 pass
Glassine: 4·5% consistency; throughput 40 tons/day, 2 pass

Specific advantages obtained with this de-flaker include: reduction in shive content; improved burst, tensile, fold and stretch values, e.g., burst and tensile up to 10% with bleached and unbleached spruce sulphite pulp in one pass; up to 155% increase in fold—tear strength remaining unaffected and increase in beating degree being negligible.

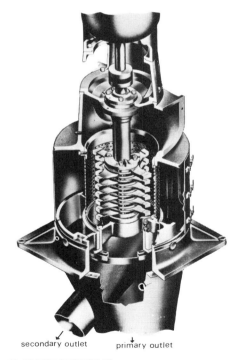

secondary outlet   primary outlet

Figure 1.29.   ELEMENTS OF THE DURAFINER

1.16.2.2 DURAFINER (Fig. 1.29)

The Durafiner is a vertical, direct-driven floor mounted machine, built with a vertical rotor shaft in stainless steel, having a series of cast steel hammers or beaters rotating in close opposition to a circular stainless steel screen. The hammers are suitably hard-faced on the leading edge. Screen perforations are $\frac{1}{8}$ or $\frac{3}{16}$ in.

Stock enters at a consistency of 2–7% and is fed into the rotor section where de-fibration takes place by the high speed rotary hammers. Accepted stock passes out through the perforated screens. Tough "elements" in the pulp progress down the screen until completely de-fibrated. Foreign matter is rejected through the secondary outlet. Suitable water injection points are arranged for secondary irrigation of the screens.

Applications include waste paper treatment—including wet strength either with steam and/or alum injection, or cold without chemical additions; esparto after cooking and rag after boiling, bagasse—in the de-pithing operation; wood pulp—in all forms; sulphite and sulphate rejects and groundwood. Bull screen rejects.

Horsepower requirements vary from 50/60 hp per ton per hour based on a 4% consistency for general waste paper grades and digested straw; to 100 hp per 3 tons per hour of these grades including wood pulp; or $1\frac{1}{2}$ tons per hour of sulphite pulp rejects.

1.17 waste paper processing systems

Of course a number of different arrangements exist for treating waste paper. The following examples are typical.

1.17.1 Clean waste paper liner system

In this relatively simple system, Fig. 1.30, paper stock is thoroughly pulped in a Hydrapulper equipped with a Vokes rotor and extracted at normal pulping consistency through 3 mm diameter perforations in an extraction plate located immediately underneath the rotor. Coaction of the Vokes rotor with the perforated extraction plate makes extraction possible through very small holes providing an effective initial separation of contaminants. One stage of centrifugal separation provides an effective further means of removal of sand, grit and other such medium to high specific gravity foreign material. One stage of further fibre reduction can be employed if necessary. Such a system provides for well de-fibred, clean stock on a continuous basis with minimum equipment requirements for use in cylinder board top liner, under liner or back liner furnishes or for other grades of paper or board which do not require the ultimate in stock cleanliness.

Paper stock thus pulped and cleaned is ready for final refining ahead of the machine chest.

1.17.2 Low brightness de-inking system

Most inks consist of pigments carried by various binders and vehicles

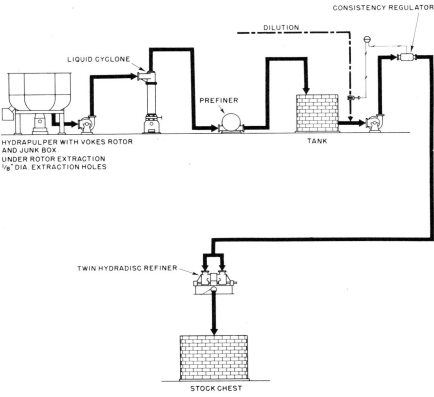

Figure 1.30. CLEAN WASTE PAPER FOR LINER SYSTEM

such as oils and waxes, latices, phenolic resins, shellac, plastisols and organosols. Where the ink vehicle can be saponified by mild alkali treatment at elevated temperature, separation and suspension of the ink from the fibres will occur.

In this simple basic system, Fig. 1.31, many grades of paper stock can be processed and the ink removed to provide a low cost, clean, low brightness pulp suitable for top or bottom boxboard liner, partial furnish for some grades of writing papers or, when using waste and over-issue news, a complete furnish for newsprint.

To increase brightness a mild, self-exhausting, self-neutralizing bleach not requiring additional equipment in the form of machinery may be added after the counterflow washers.

1.17.3 *Waste paper liner system*

This system, Fig. 1.32, substantially similar to the basic paper stock system, provides an efficient and effective means of pulping hard-to-handle waste corrugated materials for the production of bogus fluting medium or

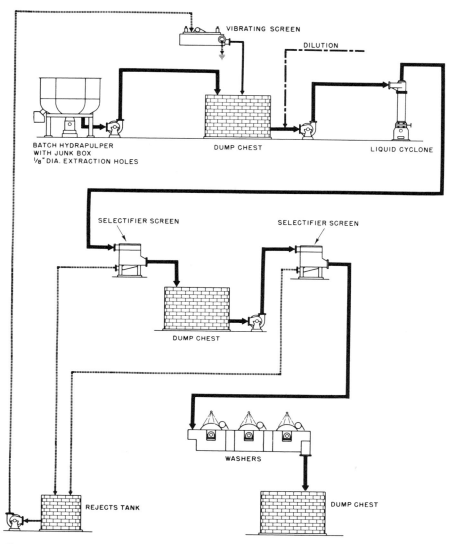

Figure 1.31. LOW BRIGHTNESS DE-INKING SYSTEM

jute linerboard. The heart of the system is the Vokes rotor Hydrapulper with extraction through 3 mm diameter perforations. When followed by medium to high gravity centrifugal separation and fine hole pressure screening, a well de-fibred clean stock is assured.

1.17.4 *Corrugated board waste system*

When it is desirable to use mixed paper stock as a furnish for cylinder board liners, this system, Fig. 1.33, provides an effective means of pulping, cleaning and screening. Unless large quantities of contaminants such as plastic coated materials, wet strength paper or other such materials are present, the contaminants and junk may be separated and removed continuously providing a well de-fibred, clean, acceptable furnish. This is made possible through the use of a Hydrapulper with Vokes rotor and under-rotor extraction through 3 mm diameter perforations, for thorough initial pulping and contaminant separation, followed by a stage of centrifugal cleaning and fine hole pressure screening, all at ideally low consistency for most effective separation of unwanted foreign materials. Continuous processing allows high productivity with minimal equipment size. Such a system provides a means of

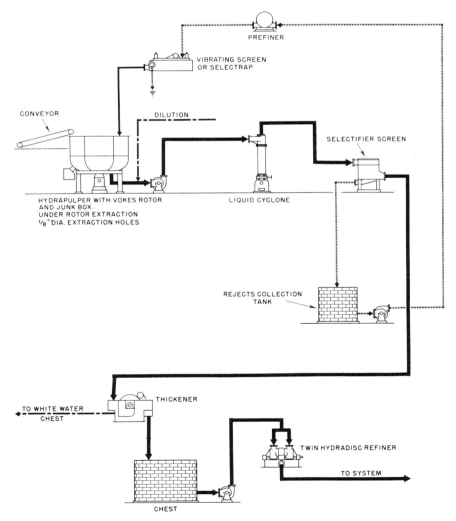

Figure 1.32.   WASTE PAPER LINER SYSTEM

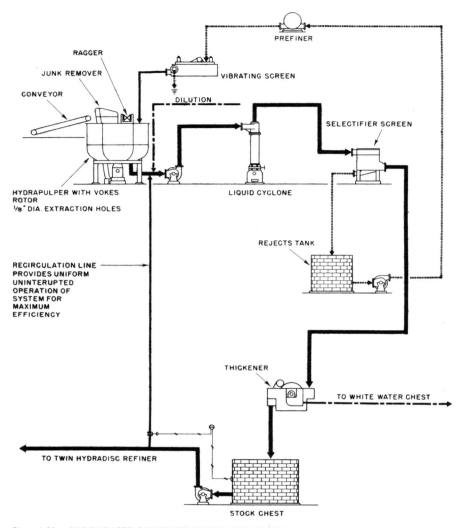

Figure 1.33. CORRUGATED BOARD STOCK PULPING SYSTEM

upgrading low grade stock to a level comparable to more expensive furnishes and thus lowers the total furnish cost. Clean stock after the thickener is ready for final refining ahead of the paper machine.

1.18 pernicious contrary removal

Waste papers and boards, according to source, contain varying amounts of contaminants. These are commonly referred to as pernicious contraries. They are listed in Table 1.4.

Table 1.4. PERNICIOUS CONTRARIES IN WASTE PAPER

Type of contrary	% Consistency	Difficulties in slushing	Sources and examples of main commercial use
Wet strength papers, i.e., treated with:		Require low pH and high temperature for dispersion	Paper towels, corrugated and solid case boards, wallpaper, coated and laminated grades. Paper cups and containers. Photographic base papers. Greeting cards, maps. Paper towels and sacks
urea formaldehyde resin	6%	pH4–4·5, at 150°F	
melamine formaldehyde	6%	pH3–3·5, at 170°F	
polyamide-epoxide	6%	pH10, at 170°F	
Latex rubber treated papers, e.g., added in the stock or as an adhesive	6%	Cannot be treated Latex as a vehicle for some coatings can be washed out, after slushing in standard de-inking system	Some papers and envelopes, pressure sensitive adhesive sealing tape and laminated grades, books and binding
Latices non-water-soluble	6% de-inking process	When alkali-soluble, will remove latices from salvaged re-usable fibres	Coated paper and board, wallpaper, containers
Non-water soluble binders and adhesives, e.g., thermoplastic and similar synthetic adhesives	6%	As above	Laminated boards and papers, show cards and bookbindings
Polythene, polyvinyl and cellulose film, i.e., viscose and acetate film	7%	Polythene film can be separated from fibres in cold pulping process and rejected	Laminated papers and boards used in bags, sacks, corrugated and solid case containers, paper cup and cartons
Waxed laminates, and wax-coated papers and boards	2½%	Fails to disperse in cold water and appears as spots in the paper—coagulates. Can be dispersed with petro-chemical diffusion	Coated and laminated grades, e.g., cartons, tubes, bread wrappings
Bitumen laminated grades	2½%	Cannot be dispersed in normal cold pulping. May be dispersed with petrochemical diffusion system	Laminated paper, multi-wall sacks and waterproof wrappings, cartons and paper tubes
Vegetable parchment	3%	Fails to disperse in cold water chemical or temp, treatment	Acid dissolved cellulose, often laminated grades, cartons
Synthetic fibres, e.g., terylene, nylon	3%	Cannot be dispersed in normal pulping methods	Bookbinders and manufacturing stationers, synthetic fibre papers maps, etc.
Metallic foils	5%	Both fibres and foil can be separated for re-use providing adhesive is soluble	Paper board coatings, printers, bookbinders, cigarette, greeting cards
Specially coated papers and boards, e.g., carbon and substitute carbon (NCR) papers	6%	Dispersable in normal cold pulping, but discolours paper stock, washing and de-inking may help	Manufacturing stationers, office wastes

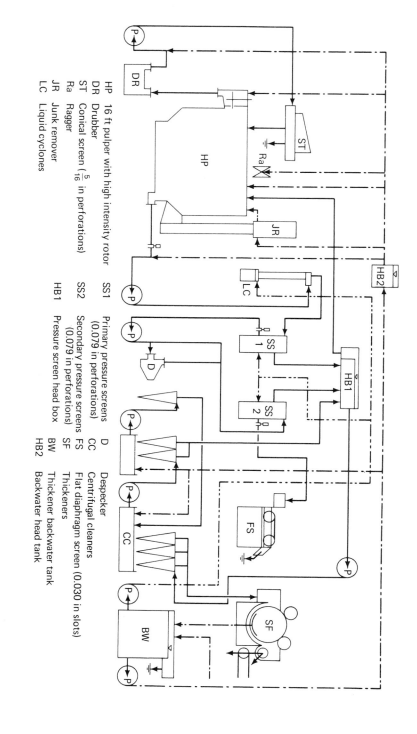

Figure 1.34. WASTE PAPER CLEANING AND SCREENING SYSTEM

HP   16 ft pulper with high intensity rotor
DR   Drubber
ST   Conical screen ($\frac{5}{16}$ in perforations)
Ra   Ragger
JR   Junk remover
LC   Liquid cyclones

SS1 Primary pressure screens
     (0.079 in perforations)
SS2 Secondary pressure screens
     (0.079 in perforations)
HB1 Pressure screen head box

D   Despecker
CC   Centrifugal cleaners
FS   Flat diaphragm screen (0.030 in slots)
SF   Thickeners
BW   Thickener backwater tank
HB2 Backwater head tank

Flow diagrams—Figs. 1.34 and 1.35—illustrate a typical mixed-waste system for removing all known evident contraries, and for a typical woodfree de-inking system for waste paper.

1.19 waste paper cleaning/screening system

Owing to the "nature" of mixed waste papers, the need for efficient cleaning and screening of the prepared fibre stock is essential in the manufacture of all but the very lowest grade and cheapest boards and even in these the acceptable degree to which "dirt" is allowed to be present in the sheet is relatively low.

A waste paper cleaning and screening arrangement typical of its type is shown in Fig. 1.34.

1.20 typical mill waste paper processing systems

Owing to the very "nature" of waste paper (particularly mixed-waste grades typically used in board mills), installations differ widely in mills throughout the world. However, modern mills generally use one or more centrifugal type disintegrators, along with accessory equipment commonly found in standard stock preparation systems. Other forms of waste paper treatment, like the De-fibrator installation, embody de-fibrator(s) in conjunction with one horizontal digester tube—screw feeder—and continuous de-watering presses.

The following is a short description of what probably represents a fairly typical modern waste paper processing installation of its kind, for the manufacture of boxboard and liner grades using a predominantly waste paper based furnish.

The particular system described includes: a Hydrapulper—flote purge system—consistency regulator (1%)—banks of liquid cyclones to remove light weight contraries—centrifugal screens—thickener for pitch dispersal under steam pressure—consistency regulator (4·5%)—dump chest—conical refiners running at 3·5% consistency—middle and back chests. This section of the system (concerned with waste paper treatment), as described, is run in conjunction with a separate and conventional stock preparation system for treating kraft pulp. In this case, the separately prepared fibre stock components are passed to a two-manifold Fourdrinier headbox—one for the liner and one for the waste paper back.

The press section of this particular machine consists of a double suction-press, a straight-through Venta-nip and an inverted Venta-nip press.

Flow diagrams are included for a typical mixed-waste system for removing all known evident contraries (Fig. 1.35) and for a typical woodfree de-inking system for waste paper (Fig. 1.36).

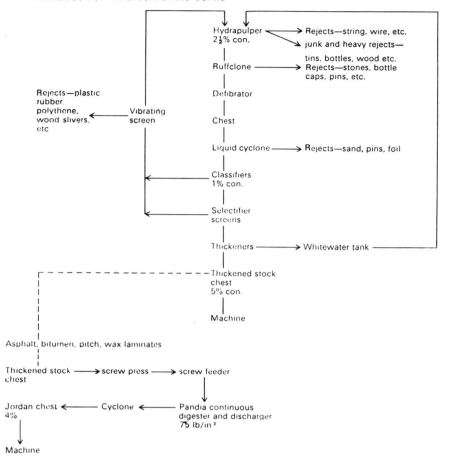

Glossary.

Ruffclone—a free vortex centrifugal cleaner. High specific gravity rejects are removed through reject box. Normally operates at 5–10 lb/in² pressure drop.

Defibrator—defibring machine for dispersing fibre bundles.

Liquid cyclone—a free vortex centrifugal cleaner. Medium and high specific gravity rejects, also plastic particles are removed through a reject box. Normally operates at 30–50 lb/in² pressure drop.

Classifier—a rotary pressurized screen.

Selectifier screen—a pressurized screen.

– – – – Alternative path for treating impregnated grades.

Figure 1.35. TYPICAL MIXED WASTE SYSTEM FOR REMOVING ALL KNOWN EVIDENT CONTRARIES

1.21 European waste paper nomenclature*

Under the framework of the European Confederation of pulp, paper and board industries, a European nomenclature for standard qualities of waste

*In international circles the term "waste paper" is being superceded by the use of the American term "paper stock", as this expression conveys more accurately the "value" of secondary fibres as an economically important source of raw material to the paper and board industry.

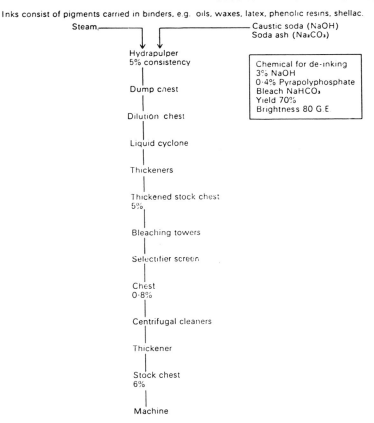

Inks consist of pigments carried in binders. e.g. oils, waxes, latex, phenolic resins, shellac.

Steam —————————————————————— Caustic soda (NaOH)
Soda ash (Na₂CO₃)

Hydrapulper
5% consistency

Dump chest

Dilution chest

Liquid cyclone

Thickeners

Thickened stock chest
5%

Bleaching towers

Selectifier screen

Chest
0·8%

Centrifugal cleaners

Thickener

Stock chest
6%

Machine

Chemical for de-inking
3% NaOH
0·4% Pyrapolyphosphate
Bleach NaHCO₃
Yield 70%
Brightness 80 G.E.

Figure 1.36. TYPICAL WOODFREE DE-INKING SYSTEM FOR WASTE PAPER

paper was published in 1967. This sets out to define the exact content and prohibitive material of the main qualities of waste papers used in the European markets. It does not list all qualities, and permissible variations are for agreement between buyer and seller. The standard grades defined represent those qualities currently offered by merchants, after sorting, grading and proper processing.

1.21.1 *Prohibited materials*

As the maximum quantity of contaminants or pernicious contraries permitted is considered differently in each country, the following definitions take into account the situation on all markets.

Prohibited materials include the following: metal; rope, glass; textiles; wood; building materials; plastics and synthetics; latex; rubbish of any description.

1.21.**2** *Improper materials or contaminants*

There are many kinds of paper/boards that have been treated in a manner that renders them unfit or noxious as a secondary fibre raw material. The presence of some of these papers or boards in waste paper would render the whole consignment unfit for use. They include for example:

Sulphurized and greaseproofed papers, wax, paraffin, bitumenized, oiled or lacquered paper and board.

Carbon papers.

Paper and board impregnated and/or coated with moisture-proof substances.

Paper and board laminated, treated or coated with plastic, bitumen or metallic foil.

Glossy paper and board, varnished or treated with synthetic or plastic varnishes or finishes, e.g., picture postcard stock.

All cellulose film, metals and metallic substances.

This list does not, of course, exhaust all possible contaminants.

1.22 **European list of standard waste paper qualities**

The qualities listed under the European standard are classified according to groups. These are: Group A—ordinary qualities, Group B—middle qualities, Group C—superior qualities, Group D—kraft qualities.

Obviously not all these groups are of interest to the paperboard industry. The groups of particular importance here include groups A, B and C.

Groups A—ordinary qualities, includes the following grades: mixed paper and boards No. 2—these consist of a mixture of various grades of paper and board, without restrictions on short fibre content; mixed papers and board No. 1—these consist of a mixture of the various qualities of paper and board and contain less than 15% short fibre papers, such as newspapers, and magazines, board cuttings. (The latter consist of new shavings or cuttings of pressed board or of mixed board free of straw board; mill wrappers.) [The latter consists of packing papers, called reel wrappers such as are used for the outer wrappings for reels, parcels or reams of new paper, free of bitumens, wax or plasticized papers.]

Group B—middle qualities, includes the following grades: old newspapers, which contain less than 5% of coloured booklets or of publicity pamphlets, free of crumpled paper; over-issue newspapers in bundles. The latter consists of unused daily newspapers, printed on white newsprint, and which do not contain more than the normal percentage of coloured illustrations, without staples, and in original packed bundles; over-issue newspapers in bales or palletized—(the same as in bundles except that these are packed in bales or on pallets). These are the grades of principal interest to paperboard producers but this group also includes mixed coloured shavings— light coloured bookbinder shavings and white pamphlets without cardboard, woodfree.

Group C—kraft qualities, includes the following grades: corrugated kraft 2. This consists of cases, sheets and shavings of corrugated board, with all liners in kraft, and only the middles in straw or waste paper, free of bitumen, wax, plasticized or wet strength paper. Corrugated kraft 1— consists of cases, sheets and shavings of corrugated board having all liners in kraft and the middles in kraft or semichemical pulp, free of bitumen wax, plasticized or wet-strength papers; used kraft bags—these consist of used kraft bags, undusted, having contained for example: building materials, fertilizers—excluding dyes or materials with a lasting odour—free of bitumen wax, plasticized or wet-strength papers; clean used kraft bags—these consist of clean used kraft bags, natural or white shade, which by previous use do not require any mechanical dusting, having contained for example: products intended for food, excluding papers impregnated by a lasting odour, free of bitumen wax, plasticized or wet-strength papers; cut-up and dusted kraft bags—these consist of used kraft bags of natural or white shade, without seam, cut-up and mechanically dusted, excluding papers which have been impregnated by dyes or a lasting odour, free of bitumen, wax, plasticized or wet-strength papers; new and used kraft bags—these consist of new and used kraft cuttings or sheets, of a natural or white shade, manufactured solely from kraft pulp or kraft waste, free of bitumen, wax, plasticized or wet-strength papers; new kraft shavings—these consist of new cuttings and waste of pure kraft pulp, of a natural shade, excluding sewn or stitched paper, strings or woven kraft—free of bitumen, wax, plasticized or wet-strength papers.

2 | raw material stock preparation

"STOCK PREPARATION" is an involved subject and one that embodies a number of considerations. In the ultimate analysis, the type of processing system(s) and equipment used will depend entirely on what kinds of papers or boards are being made and for what particular purpose or end-usage they are required.

In the manufacture of paper grades a great many more variations in preparation systems and equipment are to be found than in the case of paperboard manufacture.

The principles of stock preparation (beating/refining) remain the same. But the requirements imposed by manufacture differ greatly. Paperboard stock preparation systems are relatively simple—the principal need usually being one related to large output. Naturally some board grades enter the descriptive field of "specialities". Their manufacture dictates varying degrees of sophistication in the type of equipment and process techniques used and in the "know-how" applied. Likewise in the manufacture of papers, the many special and individualized characteristics and properties sought in such a wide range—as may extend from blotting paper and greaseproof, to sack kraft and web-offset papers, clearly calls for a vastly different set of technical and practical operating considerations.

For the reasons entered above, and in order to keep within the broad aims of this text, subject treatment in this chapter is not seen to be a comprehensive study of stock preparation techniques in common use throughout a broadly based paper and board manufacturing industry. The subject is however discussed sufficiently to put meaningful perspective to it in relation to coverage of the subject in this work.

2.1 stock preparation operations

Stock preparation can be divided conveniently into two major operations: (a) breaking down the basic raw material (pulp) into separate fibres (slush form)—except in integrated pulp and paperboard mills; (b) controlled refining ("beating") of the slushed fibres to suit the boardmaker's needs.

In both stages, fibres are subjected to mechanical treatment in the presence of water. Such treatments are carried out using appropriate type of stock preparation equipment selected from the various types of plant and machinery available for slushing and refining all types of pulps, e.g., wood, straw, bagasse, other grasses, mixed waste paper/board, etc.

2.1.1 Slushing equipment

In non-integrated paperboard mills, that must rely mainly on imported sources of pulp in semidry or dried form, there still exists a need for separate slushing equipment in which the pulp must be broken down into separate fibres. Even in some integrated mills, it is usual to use waste paper as a major fibre furnish component, and therefore disintegrating and slushing equipment is a necessary piece of equipment in the separate waste paper stock preparation line, designed to handle and process secondary fibre materials—see section 1·15.

Certainly the most common slushing equipment in use today in paperboard mills is in the form of one of a number of makes of centrifugal disintegrators.

2.2 centrifugal disintegrators

Use of centrifugal disintegrators like the Hydrapulper is now widespread. This type of equipment appears in many forms and under names like: Apmew, Hi-Low, Dino and Solvo-pulpers. These pulpers are designed for efficient slushing; no claims are made for any refining action—any increase in strength and drop in freeness which may be observed is due simply to soaking and natural "wetting" of the fibres.

Among the principal advantages of centrifugal equipment are:

Good pulp circulation.
Loosening of additives in the case of waste paper.
Removal of *contraries* in the case of waste paper (see Table 1.4, page 55).
Batch or continuous operation.
Short filling period, due to the use of whole pulp or waste paper bales.
Low power consumption for work done, e.g., 18% saving compared with other equipment, e.g., breaker.
Complete mixing of additives if added early, i.e., size, starch, loading, colour, etc.

Relatively high consistency—10–12% (batch); continuous operation—
5–6% clean stock, 1–3% dirty mixed waste paper.
Variable stock height operation without reducing efficiency.

2.2.1 *Hydrapulper*

This machine consists of a vertical bowl-shaped tank varying in diameter from 3 to 20 ft and an average depth of 10 ft.

The tank may be lined or unlined, open or closed, e.g., as in de-inking of
waste paper where heat conservation is important. Reference to Fig. 1.26,
section 1.15 shows the arrangement for continuous operation with waste
paper. The action of the multivane rotor creates a vortex of pulp circulation
as indicated by the arrows. In this manner several de-fibring actions occur
simultaneously. Capacities range from 2–6 tons with a consistency of 6–12%.

Latest developments include the introduction of an improved design high
energy rotor and bedplate, for improved slushing action—see section 1.16.1;
and a twin-rotor pulper as Fig. 2.1.

The Hydrapulper is today used successfully in treating a great variety of
furnishes, e.g., tissue, board, commercial fine paper grades, etc. It has
proved specially valuable in processing waste paper—see section 1.15.
Hydrapulpers also readily lend themselves to handling fluffy stock owing to
the fast pull of the vortex action.

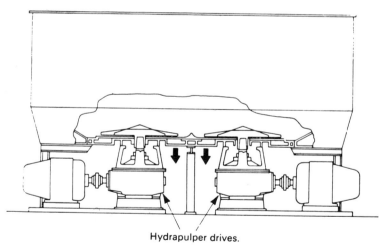

Hydrapulper drives.

Figure 2.1.   HYDRAPULPER WITH TWIN ROTOR

2.3 **stock preparation systems development**

In order to obtain maximum values of strength and performance for a
particular paper/board grade, choice of the most suitable fibre or fibre pulp
components, and treatment of the furnish, either as a whole or in part, is
critical.

In the development of modern stock preparation systems, it is interesting to compare European practice with that in the United States of America. The Europeans (especially the UK), owing to the vagaries of market demand over many years and changing consumer needs, often have had need to use one paper machine for a number of diversified paper/board qualities. The Americans, on the other hand, enjoying somewhat different marketing conditions, are able to concentrate on producing a limited range, or even one grade of paper/board per machine. This naturally influences choice in the type of stock preparation system employed.

The position is further affected from a stock preparation aspect, as seen in the growing trend towards integration in the pulp, and paper/board producing industries, especially in the USA, Canada, Scandinavia and developing countries, and more recently even in the UK. In the UK and parts of continental Europe, the economic position often necessitates the incorporation of a very much more flexible stock preparation system than would otherwise be employed, if paperboard machines were used for making a relatively small number of grades (increasing tendency is to shelve less profitable grades) and there were more integrated firms, i.e., with available indigenous resources for pulp production. The latter explains the increasing economic importance attached to the reclamation of waste paper for re-use in certain paper/board grades—largely in packaging, e.g., boxboards and containerboards. This is particularly so in Europe but applies to varying extents in all pulp producing countries owing to a too rapid increase in demand for timber and receding sources of supply.

There are probably no modern paperboard mills that are not sited in proximity to fibrous raw material sources—most are essentially integrated pulp/paperboard complexes. The prime example is kraft linerboard mills. Stock preparation equipment is relatively simple and is operated as a continuous in-line process. The formerly individualized process of "beating" using a "beating engine" has been superseded by the modern high speed refiner. These themselves are becoming more part of a total process concept of a combined pulping and stock processing operation, as for example, is particularly the case in most of the semichemical pulping techniques. Figure 2.2 shows a simple, modern process flow chart for a semichemical fluting mill using slush pulp direct from the digestion stage.

2.4 refining

"Stuff" is made ready for the board machine by a process commonly termed beating or *refining*. In practice these formerly individualized processes accomplish mixing and blending of the various paperboard making furnish materials and impart to the fibres the potential properties and characteristics desirable in the finished board.

In the "industry" today, refining is accepted as an alternative term to beating, with which it is synonymous regarding the important characteristics imparted to fibres. The important technical aspects of paperboard manufacture have actually changed very little in terms of stock preparation fundamentals. Refining, or wet fibre treatment, is still one of the most influential

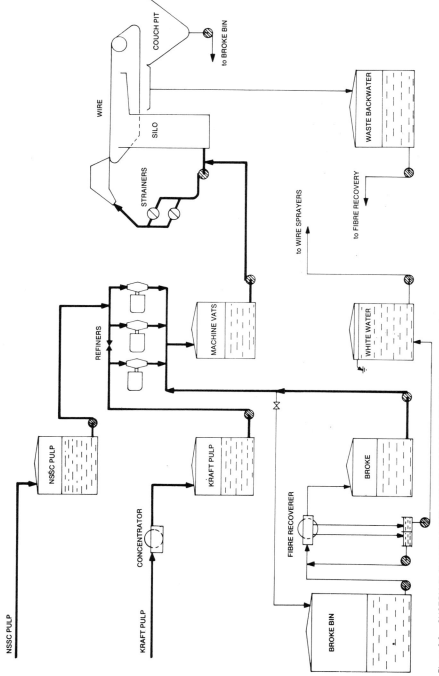

Figure 2.2.   SYSTEM FLOW FOR NSSC AND KRAFT BASED PAPERBOARD MILL

processes used initially to control "quality" of paper and board.

Of course, and not surprisingly, modern paperboard mill stock preparation systems layouts have changed a lot in recent years. This reflects both the trend towards "economy of scale" paperboard grades—where tonnage in the prime requirement, and the substantial advances made in high yield pulping processes and techniques.

The principal aim of refining today is, however, exactly as it was conceived a thousand or more years ago—except that in modern parlance we have come to call this process of fibre treatment by the term refining, rather than "beating".

Also, in those days the process was carried out in a beating machine, whereas today it is undertaken by a refiner. The aim is the same; to impart certain modifications to the structure of natural fibres to produce optimum potential bonding strength, commensurate with any specially desirable properties in the dry sheet.

Fibres used in the manufacture of papers and paperboards, when refined, undergo certain physical changes to their natural structure. This gives rise to a potential bonding affinity between cellulose surfaces in the formed web, largely by means of hydrogen bridges or bonds, see Fig. 2.7.

Refining develops sheet strength according to fibre structure. This is because the type, dimensions, composition, structure and "nature" of fibres all play important parts in respect of the characteristics/modifications they will attain during refining.

The structural differences observable in fibres from different natural sources and differences in fibre composition largely account for the respective reactions of the various fibre types to the refining action. It also helps to explain the existence of a number of variations in stock preparation techniques and layout used by mills to impart the most desirable properties in the dry sheet.

In recent years, "new" raw materials, both fibrous and non-fibrous, have been introduced to the industry and are now widely used in paperboard manufacture. Usage tends to follow the path of pulping developments—directed towards greater pulp yields and the wider usage of certain tree species and new indigenous raw materials. In addition there has been a spread in the usage of secondary fibre material—which broadly includes waste paper grades. Waste paper (paperstock)—see section 1.14—is of major economic importance to most countries engaged today in the manufacture of paperboards. Great importance is being attached to it. In consequence, such pulps have become somewhat more "tailor-made" and the need for extensive fibre treatment by the process of refining has therefore been lessened.

Fibrous raw materials of particular importance in paperboard manufacture today include:

High-yield pulps (bleached and unbleached).
Hardwoods and other short fibred pulps, e.g., straw, bagasse, etc.
Waste paper and de-inked stock.

2.4.1 *Refining and refining principles*

The object of refining is to develop a greater area available for bonding between fibres by creating conditions that allow for maximum free imbibition of water as a plasticizer (Figs. 2.3, 2.4, 2.5 and 2.6). The fibres are thereby made more flexible so they easily deform under the forces of surface tension acting during drying. The extent of the bonding thereby provided is then dependent upon the nature of the cellulose surfaces brought together. The degree of fibre bonding at the articulating crossing points of fibre fibrillae in the web depends on the local plasticity and surface topography of the fibres and the magnitude of the forces in the vicinity.

One of the most important factors concerns the extent of fibre surface available for bond formation—see section 2.4.1.1.

The primary fibre wall, because it does not swell, has a certain restraining effect on the take up of water by the fibre. However, owing to its thinness it probably has less restraint on swelling than S1. In chemical pulp, partial removal and weakening of the primary wall during digestion and bleaching help in its complete elimination during the initial stages of refining and may well account for the noticeable rise in sheet strength values by hastening take up of water in the layers S1 and S2. Following the removal of the primary wall, there takes place a removal of successive lamellae of the outer layer of the secondary wall S1, during refining. Semichemical processed pulp fibres behave somewhat differently when refined, which is in accordance with the different chemical treatment they have undergone—see section 1.2.2/1.5.

Swelling achieved by internal fibrillation is brought about by fibre flexing during the early stages of beating and causes a rupture of some internal hydrogen bonds, notably in the middle secondary wall S2. In consequence, there is an intake of water molecules by the fibre as the structure begins to open up. This imbibition of water causes an increase in the *specific volume*

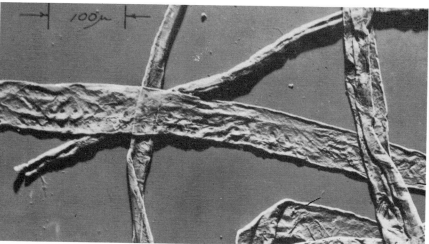

Figure 2.3.   UNREFINED SOFTWOOD FIBRES

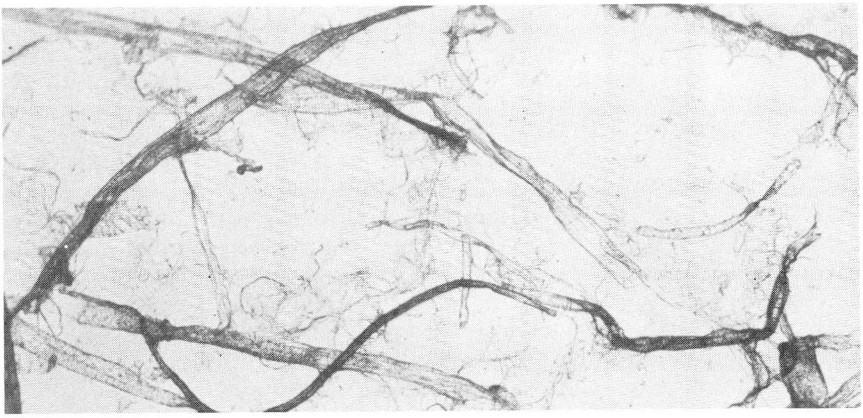

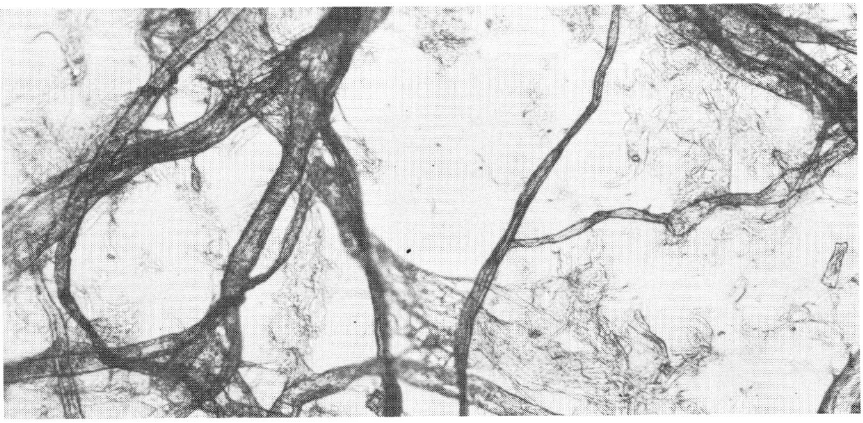

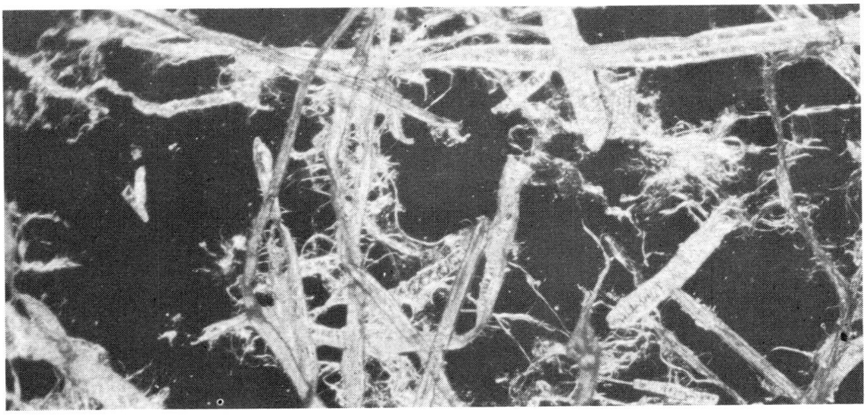

Figures 2.4, 2.5, 2.6. REFINED FIBRES
In these three pictures, the effect of refining on fibre structure in contrast to Fig. 2.3 is quite apparent.

of the fibre as a result of swelling in the fibre walls. In itself, the increase in specific volume of the fibres is unimportant. Its significance lies in an intake of water, which exerts a plasticizing effect—*internal lubrication*—in the fibre walls allowing the fibre to conform to the forces of surface tension on drying. The fibre wall principally involved is the middle secondary wall, S2, which, owing to its more highly ordered cellulose formation, readily allows of opening up. By virtue of its helical fibril winding, which is in an almost axial direction, S2 on drying is able to assume relatively stress free positions; consequently, extensive hydrogen bonding is free to take place, providing the surfaces are favourable.

A desirable effect of refining should allow for maximum entanglement of fibres in the web, owing to improved positioning which affords greater opportunities for bonding. Evidence indicates that mechanical entanglement of fibres contributes significantly to sheet strength—providing the adjacent fibre surfaces in the web can be kept close enough to allow the necessary physio-chemical bond to occur during microfibrillar cohesion, subsequent to the removal of the entrained water during drying. Restriction of surface motion of the fibres in a web reduces the effectiveness of the mechanical factors involved during formation and consolidation, e.g., wet pressing. If the greater bonding opportunities provided for by mechanical entanglement are to be effective, therefore, a degree of plasticity–internal fibrillation must be induced in the fibre structure.

The ability of cellulose fibres to fibrillate internally is directly related to their water-sorption properties. Internal fibrillation is greatly assisted by the presence of hemicelluloses, as these are able to accelerate the plastic phase in the fibre structure and increase its flexibility owing to the additional intake of water molecules into the structural walls of the fibre as beating progresses. This produces increased frictional resistance of the fibres towards displacement after formation and wet pressing with consequent failure of bonds on stressing during drying.

The important effects of refining on fibre structure may best be summarized by quoting Borruso, who asserts on experimental evidence that:

> The increase in specific surface varies in extent with the pulp and progresses with beating.
>
> The effective specific volume increases rapidly at first with beating to reach a constant maximum value later.
>
> No relationship exists between the amount of increase in specific surface and strength of the sheet.
>
> The effective specific volume includes water taken up in wetting and fixed fibres, so preventing drainage through them.
>
> A significant correlation exists between effective specific volume and strength characteristics developed by refining, particularly in the first stages (see above).

2.4.1.1 IMPORTANCE OF FIBRE SURFACES

There are many different surfaces exhibited by papermaking fibres. In the past possibly too much attention has been focused on the external surface of the primary wall, in relation to its restraining effect on fibre bond development. Again, emphasis has been laid on the contributing effects of mechanical entanglement of microfibrils holding fibres together in the sheet, sheet strength thus being variably attributed to fibre felting and hemicellulose content. That these factors, and many allied with paperboard machine performance, e.g., consolidation of the web during wet pressing and drying, are very closely associated with the development of dry sheet strength is evident. It is clear, however, that these are not the most positive factors responsible for the forces holding fibres together in the sheet. Sheet formation is complex and consists of a collection of somewhat inextricably combined factors, each related to the others and to the whole. More important than the absolute strength of the individual fibres is the relationship between fibre structure and the bonding potential of its exposed surface.

When plant cellulose is digested chemically there takes place, to varying degrees, the removal of lignin and hemicelluloses. In this manner the structure is considerably weakened as the cellulose fibre becomes purified.

The effect of intermediate drying on the structure of the fibre results in collapse of the cell wall, caused by the removal of water; this sets up strong adhesion forces largely through hydrogen bonding between articulating areas of microfibrils, Fig. 2.7. The whole cellular structure takes on a different appearance according to the restraint on shrinkage imposed during microfibrillar cohesion. Internal bonding of this nature produces partial irreversible *hornification* of the fibre structure, which explains the effect on pulp properties of partial intermediate drying of pulp for transport reasons.

In order to rediscover fresh areas over which bonding can take place, a refining action is necessary to separate the closely knit fibrillar strands of the cell wall. The principal action sought in beating is mechanical flexion of fibres.

2.4.1.2 EXPOSED FIBRE WALL SURFACE

When fibres in the formed web are brought together during the stages of drying, the strength of the bond formed between them will depend on the nature of their contact surfaces. In turn, the surface of a fibre is related to the type and degree of pulping and the modifications imparted to its structure during refining.

During pulping, purification of the fibres begins with selective action of the chemical liquor for lignin, concentrated mostly in the primary and outer secondary walls. Thus, exposure of the fibre surface by the chemical action of liquors in the digestion and bleaching processes is of particular importance. The exposed surface of a fibre refers to the area of fibre surface from which the primary wall has been removed, taken as a percentage of the total surface.

2.4.2 *Effect of pulp properties on refining*

WHY DO PULPS DIFFER? Pulps differ widely in refining response because of variations in fibre morphological features, chemical constitution and physical structure. In general, individual pulp behaviour depends on the following fibre characteristics:

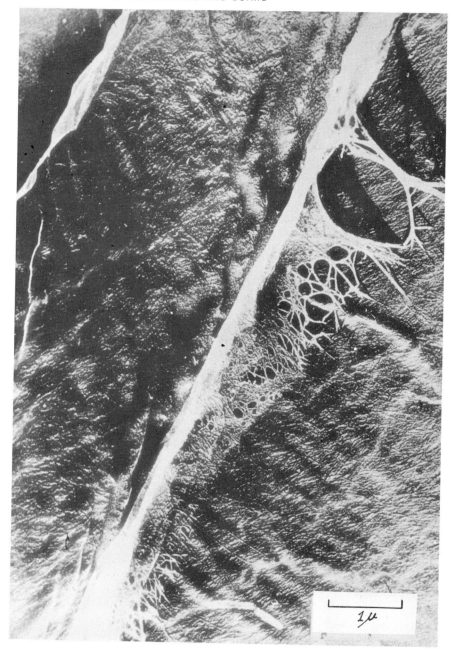

Figure 2.7. MICROFIBRILS BONDING TWO FIBRE SURFACES

MORPHOLOGICAL Length stiffness and cell wall thickness.
PHYSICAL Cellulose purity (DP) and individual fibre strength.
CHEMICAL Presence of hemicelluloses and modified lignin.
PHYSIO-CHEMICAL Swollen, imbibed condition.

Morphological. Individual fibre strength predominantly influences tearing resistance. In a single virgin pulp furnish, fibre length may be taken as a criterion of tearing strength. With mixed pulp furnishes, this may not apply, because one fibre component may absorb more beating—this largely depends on fibre surface and strength, both properties being influenced by the pulping process. Consequently, it is unwise to predict results of a mixed furnish based on the strength values for the separate components, either when beaten separately or together.

Although fibre length is of definite importance in the development of certain paper properties, primarily as regards initial wet strength and tear resistance, it is probable that in general the importance of fibre length has been over-estimated. It is likely that differences in fibre stiffness play a larger rôle from the papermaking viewpoint. Stiffness is dependent on the presence of fibrous constituents, and cell wall thickness in relation to fibre length and diameter.

Cell wall thickness largely accounts for the pre-drying effect on fibres. Hardwoods have thick cell walls in relation to their diameter and resist collapse better than thinner walled softwoods. Collapsed fibres generally impart low opacity, bulk (air space) and high general strength to papers, owing to the large total area available for bonding. The cylindrical fibres of hardwoods yield papers of lower general strength, high bursting strength, bulk, opacity, absorbency and air permeability.

Fibre form (dependent on pulp yield) is important because of its influence on sheet strength properties. The degree of *passive* and *active* fibre segments determines fibre conformability in sheet during drying and consequently affects the stress/strain relationships in the sheet (modulus of elasticity)—see sections 6.6.**3**/6.12/6.13.

Physical—Fibre cellulose purity—degree of polymerization (DP)—denotes the average length of the cellulose units comprising a fibre and affects individual fibre strength properties such as tear and tensile. Pulps behave basically according to fibre nature and method of isolation from the plant. Fibres of the same origin, when pulped by different processes, exhibit different refining properties and sheet characteristics. For example, when other conditions remain equal, sulphite processed fibres develop tear and tensile strength values more quickly during refining in contrast to sulphate processed fibres. Sulphate pulps beat more slowly, but develop higher overall sheet strength. This is largely the effect of structural modifications to the surface of the fibres during digestion.

Chemical—Hemicelluloses accelerate fibre swelling according to their state and location in the fibre walls. Their presence in pulps is a criterion of the nature of the pulping treatment, since this alters the surface structure of fibres. In every.pulp, there is an optimum hemicellulose content at which maximum general sheet strength occurs. Lignin affects fibre strength development adversely by limiting swelling, and consequently bonding strength potential.

Physio-chemical—Refining behaviour of pulps depends on the swollen condition of fibres. Pre-dried fibres lose this swelling ability; in the case of wood, by 21–38% of the slush value, which accounts for a certain inferiority of dried pulps. Absorption of water during beating is 16–31% cotton fibre, 25–30% for wood.

Wetting of pulp fibres is indicated by an increase in effective specific volume of the fibres; fibrillation by its greater specific surface. Refining produces more of an increase in fibre surface than volume, as wetting is limited to the exposed fibre surface. The specific surface varies in extent with the pulp and progresses with beating. No relationship exists between the amount of specific surface and sheet strength. A significant correlation exists, however, between effective specific volume and sheet strength developed by refining. Effective specific volume (wetting) increases during initial refining to reach a constant value.

2.5 refiner requirements

Modern paperboard mill manufacturing requirements demand that refining be a "flexible" operation. Improvement in forming machines, drying capacity, faster pulp digestion processes, continuous unit operation and consumer demand have forced the traditional beater into retirement, greater efficiency and better control having become the sleeping partners of flexibility (Fig. 2.8).

Figure 2.8. 441 BAUER DISC REFINERS IN FLUTING MILL STOCK PREPARATION PLANT

Flexibility in this sense has different interpretations according to the needs of the paperboard mill. It can mean making a number of paperboards on one board machine a day; or to a large board mill, say making kraftliner board, it means simply a variation in tonnage.

There are a number of design varieties of refiners available on the market today. These may broadly be distinguished as cone refiners and disc refiners.

Each is distinctive in what it can do, how it is best applied and the extent of its versatility. Disc refiners, for reasons covered later, are today used widely in paperboard mills.

Design of refining equipment in the last decade has changed substantially. This is largely owing to a commercial need for improved efficiency, in terms of: lower specific power consumption, greater automation and closer manufacturing control with less labour.

Refining is dependent in most cases on the following important variables:

> Type and "nature" of fibres.
> Consistency of stock.
> Rate of flow.
> Width and material of refining surfaces.
> Width and depth of refiner inter-bar grooves.
> Angle of refiner "working" surfaces.
> Peripheral speed of moving elements.

REFINER VARIABLES AND QUALITY CONSIDERATIONS. All refiners, regardless of design, impart treatment to stock through the action created between two surfaces, separated by a fibre film which essentially acts as a lubricant. The treatment received by stock in refiners is governed by several refiner variables:

> Type of refiner.
> Type of bar filling.
> Horsepower applied.
> Revolutions per minute.

And by pulp variables:

> Nature of the furnish.
> Refiner throughput.
> Consistency of stock.

In selecting a refiner, these factors must all be analysed in keeping with the paper/board end product requirements. Once the choice has been made, only two independent variables remain: flow rate and horsepower applied. Consistency is certainly important, but this may quite well be considered along with flow rate. Interestingly enough this "fact of life" holds true for all refining mechanisms.

REFINER "TACKLE". It appears likely that the fluid mechanics inside a refiner involve a fourfold process:

1 Localized preliminary de-watering of fibre flocks and bundles gathered between approaching bars, becoming sufficiently compacted that further mechanical pressure expels water from this localized fibre mass. Consistency at the localized zone is expected to be higher than the general mass.

2 Mechanical pressure of approaching bars becomes sufficiently high to exceed the structural elastic limit of fibres and further water is expelled.

3 A shearing movement causes flexure, compression and sometimes rupture of some fibres.

4 Release of the mechanical pressure, allowing re-imbibition of water into the ruptured fibre structure. This is followed by or coincident with local turbulence, which disperses the "flock" into the general mass flow.

When in the second stage the mechanical pressure is insufficient to exceed the elastic limit of the flock, the fibres will spring back without any physical change. The term "flock" is used in preference to the general term "fiberage" as the latter suggests a continuous coverage of the tackle elements. This apparently does not occur and only localized, forming, dispersing and re-forming of flocks in closely spaced small areas is believed to take place.

2.6 disc refiners

The disc refiner was originally developed to handle coarse fibres, such as groundwood, semichemical pulps and pulp reject material. Today various makes of disc refiners are available, either with two or four disc assemblies. More recently much attention has been focused on design of disc working area, such that disc refiners are now used effectively on a wide range of stocks for many paper/board grades. Disc refiners have a low load requirement and consume less horsepower than conical type refiners per net fibre treatment. They also have a smaller working area than an equivalent sized Jordan, high speed refiner or wide-angle refiner (see Fig. 2.9). Specific load

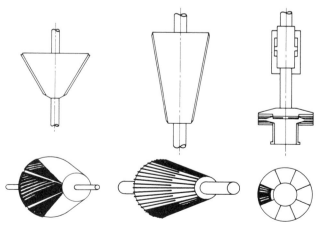

Figure 2.9.   REFINER WORKING AREAS   Wide angle, conical and disc.

capacity ranges from 2–12 hpt/day (horsepower tons per day). The upper limit is dependent on the ability of the fibres in the refining pressure zone to support this level without collapsing and allowing the disc plates to come into contact.

Weak pulps capable of supporting only 5 hpt/day, but requiring perhaps 8 hpt/day to produce the desired sheet characteristics, would have to be treated in a multiple-pass system with two refiners connected in series.

Pulps are indicated in descending order of specific load carrying ability, for common grades.

> Unbleached softwood krafts.
> Bleached softwood krafts and sulphites.
> High yield pulps and waste papers (paperstock).
> Hardwood pulps and shoft fibred krafts.

Disc refiners also develop freeness drop (rise in °SR) at lower power consumption than conical type refiners. In addition, they are seen to cut the fibre less, an important observation in the manufacture of many paperboard grades.

With disc refiners, it is important to maintain close proximity between discs. In a conical type refiner centrifugal force tends to move the stock into the stator. In a disc, the effect is to send stock towards its outer periphery. Any "backing-off" of a disc will cause a large quantity of fibres to pass through the working area untreated so it is customary to operate discs in the loaded area of 80–100%.

2.6.1 Disc refiner types and sizes

Although early disc refiners employed one refining zone only, made up of one stationary backing disc and one rotating disc, there are now available a number of makes that incorporate two refining zones with two backing discs mounted on non-rotating sliding heads and two rotating discs mounted one on each side of the rotating centre disc.

The advantage of the latter design is that twice the refining area and power is available on almost the same floor space, driven from only one motor.

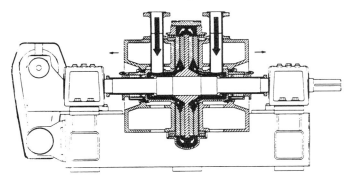

Figure 2.10. DUAL FLOW DISC REFINER
This type of refiner is normally available in sizes between 50–100 cm disc diameter.

Some use a straight-through flow pattern, others apply the principle of divided or dual flow.

Figure 2.10 illustrates stock flow and principle of design of one of the modern disc refining units. This type of dual-flow disc refiner is available in sizes varying 50–100 cm diameter discs, generally in the connected power range from about 115 hp to 12,000–14,000 hp.

2.6.1.1 DISC REFINER VARIABLES

A number of process factors enter into refining. An important one is the "toughness" of the individual fibre. A high-yield softwood kraft pulp will accommodate, and certainly require, a great deal of bar-to-bar pressure (or horsepower at same speed and disc diameter) for a given dry-sheet strength development. Equal bar-to-bar pressure on hardwood sulphite pulp would however result in considerable fibre damage—probably with complete fibre structure breakdown. Some fibre breakdown can be viewed in the centre of Fig. 2.3.

Other important process variables include the relative speed between disc plates. Effective speeds of less than 1,200 m (4,000 ft/m) with equal bar-to-bar pressure appears to give a predominantly fibre cutting action with less fibrillation. Speeds of around 1,500 m (5,000 ft/m), which is normal on slush pulp (never dried), seems to give a good balance between control of fibre length and fibrillation. At speeds over 1,800 m (6,000 ft/m) it is difficult to cut and de-fibring predominates.

Apparent bar-to-bar pressure and the (currently unknown) effects of hydraulic shear are important factors connected with high relative disc speed.

Disc refiner bars are normally set at an angle to the radius. The angle may be varied. Normally it is 15–20°, but can vary 7.5–30°. Discs can be run in either "hold-back" or "throw-out" position. With the bar angle trailing, a centrifugal pumping effect is obtained and is effectively the "throw-out" position. Running in the opposite direction, the bars tend to "hold-back" stock flow. These factors give measurable differences in refiner performance.

In commercial operation it is found that disc plates with bars at an angle of 22.5–25° to the radius run in "hold-back" position give a significant increase in bursting strength and reduction in tearing strength, at equal freeness, in contrast to plates with a lesser bar angle. Operation in "hold-back" position apparently contributes towards slightly more fibre cutting (measured by comparable bursting and tearing strengths), than in measured "throw-out" operation.

The designed contact area configuration of disc plates (these are made up of segments whose number depends on size and disc diameter) varies somewhat. Current industry belief is that a very wide range of disc configurations is unnecessary. Also apparent is that a few basic disc designs with bar and channel (groove) widths varying 3.1–6.5 mm ($\frac{1}{8}$–$\frac{1}{4}$ in) will provide all the necessary flexibility.

The early disc refiner concept only extended to an application in the "economy of scale" grades such as linerboard, but design changes now make these refiners ideal for use in nearly all paper and paperboard stock preparation processes.

In some linerboard mills, disc refiners are used as the *only* fibre processing treatment. In most cases, however, standard conical refiners (Jordans) are used for the final freeness (fibre length) control.

A typical arrangement in a mill producing fluting medium from 65% waste paper in a mixture with NSSC pulp and box shop waste, is the following example in Table 2.1.

Table 2.1. TYPICAL STOCK PREPARATION EQUIPMENT IN USE IN FLUTING MEDIUM MILL

Equipment	Applied power
despecker (one)	60 kW
conical refiners (none)	0
disc refiners (one)	135 kW
Jordan (one)	40 kW
output day	112,000 lb
Concora	2·3 kg

2.7 linerboard stock refining

Typical of stock preparation techniques in North American kraft linerboard mills is this description.

The mill prepares its pulp using two vertical stationary type digesters according to flow diagram Table 2.2. One is for production of base stock, the other for top liner stock. Stock from the top liner blow tank is pumped directly to pressurized hot stock screens using 2 mm (0·085 in) plates. Stock from the base sheet blow tank passes through fibrillizers where it is processed, to partially reduced chipped form. Stock is now pumped to two hot stock Sprout-Waldron twin-flo 0·9 m (34 in) refiners pulling 450 hp, 600 rev/min

Table 2.2. FLOW DIAGRAM OF LINERBOARD MILL IN USA

```
                    Top liner stock        Base sheet stock
                      Digester                Digester
                         /                       /
                      Blow tank               Blow tank
                         /                       /
screen rejects  ←  Hot stock screens    Hot stock screens  →  screen rejects
                         /                       /
                  Brown stock washers    Brown stock washers
                         /                       /
                      Storage                 Storage
                         /                       /
                   Machine chest            Consistency
                         /                       /
                    Consistency              Refiners
                         /                       /
                     Refiners              Machine chest
                         /                       /
rejects     ←        Screens               Consistency
                         /                       /
                  Machine headbox            Refiners
                                                 /
                                             Screens      →    rejects
                                                 /
                                         Machine headbox
```

motors fitted with electro-mechanical plate positions. Pulp at 740–780°csf issue from the refiners to hot stock screens with 3 mm (0·110 in) plates.

Base stock refining takes place in two Sprout-Waldron twin-flo refiners operating in parallel running with 700 hp motors at 600 rev/min. Throughput is 280–300 tons per day.

Top liner refining using pulp at 750–775°csf takes place in a single 0·9 m (34 in) twin-flo control refiner with a 700 hp, 600 rev/min motor. In the development of a 425–450°csf top liner stock (350°csf or 26 lb liner) refiner power input averages about 10 hpd/tons.

3 | manufacture of paperboards and boards

3.1 paperboard terminology

"**Paper**" is generally termed *board* when its substance exceeds 220 g/m². Paperboard is a term used as a subdivision of paper (general term), the other being *paper* (specific term). However, the distinction between paper and paperboard is not sharp. Paperboard as a term is usually used to signify that the paper material is of heavier basis weight than paper as such, and is likely to be thicker and more rigid.

In most countries paperboard is usually classed as such when its thickness exceeds 0·30 mm (0·012 in). One exception is the UK which uses a lower limit of 0·25 mm (0·010 in).

Another trade exception concerns traditional nomenclature. For example, drawing paper (cartridge) in excess of 0·30 mm thickness is still referred to as *paper*. Yet corrugating medium under 0·30 mm [it is usually 0·225 mm (0·009 in)] is classified as *paperboard*.

Board, perhaps with certain recognized exceptions, is commonly used as a general term to broadly distinguish between paper (general term) and paperboard (general term). "*Cardboard*" is still used in this latter sense but today has no specific meaning.

In most cases of common terminology board is a synonym for paperboard. For example, trade practice dictates that paperboard for use in the manufacture of corrugated containers (boxes) is called container *board* rather than container *paperboard*. They are here synonymous terms. Likewise, in the case of the term *boxboard*. This term refers to paperboard used in the manufacture of folding cartons.

Clearly there is room for confusion in usage of these terms, but generally in the industry they are used in context, and according to the industry and the individual doing the talking the term is usually understood. However, there are broad classes used and these are as follows.

(1) *Container board*, used for corrugated and solid fibreboard boxes.
(2) *Boxboard*—this is further divided into:
    (a) *folding boxboard*, (b) *special foodboard*, (c) *setup (rigid) boxboard*.
(3) Other special types of board such as *building board, tube board, etc.*

The use of board as a specific term is generally applied to corrugated board. This is an abbreviation of corrugated *fibreboard*. Fibreboard is a term used to refer to corrugated fibreboard and solid fibreboard used to manufacture transit containers. In the case of corrugated board the term is quite clear. However, solid board is a term that could easily be confused in its usage out of context, with certain paperboard grades used in folding carton manufacture. These include multi-ply paperboards which differ in the pulp components used in the furnish of the various plies, in contrast to a similar paperboard for folding carton conversion manufactured from one basic pulp component (usually a bleached pure pulp). In the latter case the term solid board is frequently used to distinguish between this and the multi-ply construction referred to.

Author's note: Generally throughout this text the author has chosen to use the term paperboard and board in much the same way as it is used in the industry and also for reasons of ease of reading. This is in preference to using consistently the one term *paperboard*—with which, as already explained, board is largely synonymous within this text.

3.2 **sheet formation: factors affecting it**

Sheet formation is complex. Suspensions of fibres in the concentrations usually employed in boardmaking can be considered as three dimensional networks, more or less heterogeneous in structure and endowed with special rheological properties. The internal cohesion of these networks in water determines the forming properties of the pulp and the properties of the moist sheet so formed. The three groups of factors having a determining influence can be regarded as the organization of the fibres in the network, the geometrical and mechanical properties of these fibres (in particular, their conformability/deformability) and the surface properties of fibres that determine the transmission of stresses between the fibres.

"Quality" and "strength" of paper/board as controlled by the forming process depend on:

> *Degree of fibre treatment.*
> *Degree of fibre dispersion.*
> *Degree of fibre orientation.*

Factors that predominantly control sheet formation involve:

1 Machine headbox conditions.
2 Hydrodynamic conditions in the approach-flow system and stock outlet.
3 State and *form* of fibres, section 2.4.**2**.

Irrespective of the designs and configurations of the paperboard machine, all the above factors hold good. Generally, therefore, taking these points in order, the following observations can be made.

Important headbox conditions involve: pressure head of stock; stock consistency; the point and angle of stuff impingement/deposition on the forming wire; slice setting and wire forming arrangements—see section 3.4.**1**.

Accurate regulation of the stock head is always essential to prevent poor sheet formation. This observation applies in a general sense to all forming processes. It is particularly apparent on Fourdrinier machines, where too low a stock head causes pronounced machine-direction flocculation and *worming*; too great a head produces sheet irregularities. Consistency changes in the stock cause a variation in flow rate—low velocity causes fibre floc formation and the deposition of mineral fillers and fibre fines. High stock velocity creates eddies and secondary flows, giving rise to "streaks" and other sheet defects. Consistency (of stock) is an important variable in all paper/board making processes. The obvious differences in the formation characteristics of single wire, double wire, and cylinder-type machines, lays varying emphasis on these above noted points.

Irrespective of the machine type and its individual formation characteristics, *fibre form* is a particularly overall significant factor.

3.2.**1** *Fibre form*

Fibre form is important because it is influential in the development of stress/strain characteristics in the sheet. Fibre form is dependent on pulp *yield* and is therefore directly related to the chemical pulping processes—see section 1.2. Fibre form itself directly influences sheet formation characteristics and in consequence dry-sheet strength properties, and also several of the properties that determine many intangible factors introduced in assessing so-called practical machine "runnability" in converting operations.

Sheet formation is complex. More important than the absolute strength of the individual fibres is the relationship between the fibre structure/form and the bonding potential of its exposed surface in the freshly formed web. *The nature of the surface of a fibre is related to the type and degree of chemical pulping it has undergone and the modifications imparted to its surface during beating.* The ultimate degree of fibre bonding in the formed web depends on the local plasticity and surface topography of the fibres plus the magnitude of the forces in the vicinity. Both these observations are illustrated in Figs. 3.1, 3.2 and 3.3. They show transmitted light and scanning electron micrographs of semichemical and kraft fibres before and after refining.

In summary, the technological factors of major importance involved in paperboard formation may ultimately be traced directly to:

D

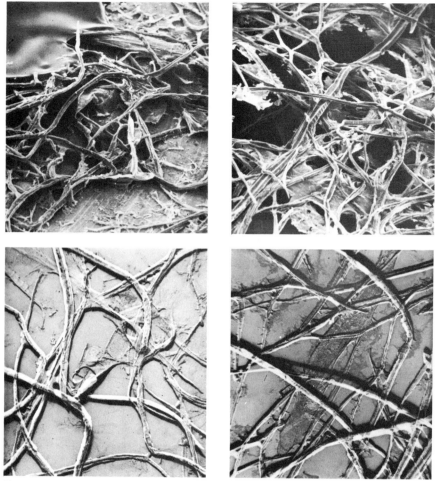

Figure 3.1.   NEVER DRIED BIRCH SEMICHEMICAL PULP
Scanning electron (a + b) and transmitted light (c + d) micrographs of never-dried birch semichemical pulp show clearly the increasing flexibility (conformability) of the fibre upon disintegration (a) and beating (b). The exposed surfaces of such fibres and the fines produced differ morphologically from those of chemical pulps. Thus, the bonding of fibres of semichemical pulps can arise between surfaces of very different composition and physical organization. Mag.× 144.

1   Fibre form (dependent on pulp yield). The degree of *passive* and *active* fibre segments determines fibre conformability in the sheet (during drying) and consequently affects the stress/strain relationships in the sheet (modulus of elasticity)—see sections 6.6.**3**/6.12/6.13.

2   Fibre surface (related to type and degree of chemical pulping in terms of exposed fibre-wall surface.

3   Fibre structure (modifications imparted during refining).

These technological factors are found to have varying degrees of practical implications in the various paperboard converting operations.

Figure 3.2.   NEVER DRIED KRAFT FIBRES
Scanning electron (a+b) and transmitted light (c+d) micrographs of never-dried kraft fibres. Compare with Figs. 3.1. Mag. ×144.

3.3 development behind modern boardmaking machines

It is as well, firstly, to recognize that there is a reason lying behind the different approaches to board manufacturing methods, as seen in the development between North America and Europe.

Multi-ply paperboard manufacture in its early days, before its explosion in the late 1930–40 era, was a relatively crude and simple process. A number of installations consisted of a Fourdrinier machine with a secondary headbox placed somewhere along the Fourdrinier wire. (There are still some of these installations running today. They are, however, more commonly to be found in Europe.)

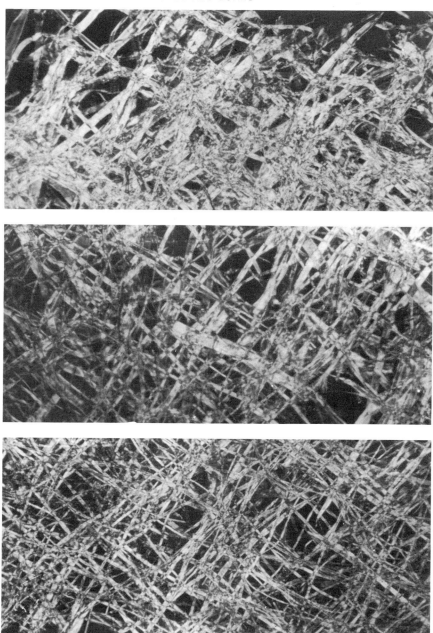

Figure 3.3 (a), (b) and (c).   FIBRE DISTRIBUTION

The distribution of fibres and manner in which they intermesh in the formed web, differs according to type, form, preparation, etc., as may be seen here with 100% wood fibres—50/50% wood and straw fibres, and 100% straw fibres.

Not only were these early machines crude, but the web-combining process was also largely one of "luck". In order to overcome fibre conglomeration and drainage problems, manufacturers resorted to using virtually unbeaten stock for the body of the sheet. Initially formed on the Fourdrinier wire, this body ply then received a top fibre layer (from the secondary headbox) of more heavily beaten top liner stock. As still with existing machines of this type, water from the newly deposited fibre suspension must drain through the already formed fibre layer. In other words, the Fourdrinier machine designed for the manufacture of paper somewhat suddenly found itself trying to cope with and accommodate the manufacture of multi-layer paperboards. Thus it was, that it took nearly 100 years before paperboard was made on a Fourdrinier machine.

While a growth in paperboard was taking place in the United States, Europe was facing difficulties occasioned by lack of the large production orders more readily available to the larger American paperboard machines. European manufacturers therefore turned their attention more towards improving their existing machines, both in speed and formation. The movement towards improving formation was especially prominent in those countries relying most on the use of secondary fibre (waste) materials. Here the basic need was to cover a predominantly waste fibre body with the thinnest possible layer of pure virgin fibre. This need was actually greatest in the 15 years after the end of the Second World War. In both Europe and the United States, cartonboard output trebled during this period, although the build-up was felt a little later in Europe. In many cases, European production was met by the use of combined Fourdrinier machines, i.e., Fourdrinier-formed liner followed by subsequent layers (plys) formed on cylinder machines of various types—see also section 3.4.1.13.

In Europe today, there exists a wide variety of combination paperboard and board machines. Many of them are "mongrel" constructions that well serve their purpose however. Mainly as a result of the early efforts to produce combined paperboards at high speeds, there later appeared a crop of "current" forming devices such as are described later. This development is probably just now reaching its zenith.

The outcome over a long period of the many and varied efforts to produce the ideal paperboard-forming machine (many of which took place almost simultaneously) is that in recent years certain notable "breakthrough" machinery developments have taken place. Here one may specifically mention the Inverform, Ultra Former; and although it is still early yet, in terms of experience, the Verti-Forma, and Papriformer. There are others.

3.4 boardmaking operations/methods

The earliest machines used in the manufacture of paperboards were Fourdrinier and cylinder machines—hence the origin of the term "cylinder boards".

Today, a number of commercial wet processes exist for the manufacture of single and multi-ply paperboard and board. They principally are: Fourdrinier: single or multi-wires; cylinder—multi-vats; formers—Rotiformer,

Ultra former, etc.; combination machines—Fourdrinier and combined vat machines with MG cylinder, pre- and after-cylinders, etc.; double wire drainage devices--Inverform; and others.

Dry boardmaking processes include the so-called "after-processes" of converting. These embody operations of pasting, laminating, corrugating, etc.

In this sense "dry" is not to be confused with current developments by which paper and paperboards can be "formed" using never-wet fibres.

Descriptions of the above principal methods of paperboard manufacture now follow.

3.4.1 *Modern forming methods*

In the field of board technology particular attention is being focused on improved methods of sheet formation. This especially applies to multi-ply webs, mainly on account of:

Improved economies of increased production.

Use of lower grade secondary fibres, e.g., waste paper, in certain paper and board grades—(container and folding carton grades), particularly for middle plies.

Probability of using new raw materials to improve paper/board properties—e.g., synthetic fibre stocks or "blends" in individual plys.

As a means of enhancing sheet properties by control of degree of order in individual fibrous layers to form a "square" sheet—more isotropic.

Figure 3.4.   MULTI-FOURDRINIER COMPLEX AND COMBINED CYLINDER-VAT MACHINE
Two or more Fourdrinier wire-parts run in series, with web consolidation at a suitable point.

FOURDRINIER MACHINE. A number of Fourdrinier machine configurations are in use in the manufacture of single- and multi-ply paperboards. They are either by means of a multi-Fourdrinier complex (two or more Fourdrinier wire-parts running in series, with web consolidation at a suitable point, Fig. 3.4), or by combination of Fourdrinier wire-parts with conventional type cylinder-mould vat sections (and more latterly with the newer formers). Fourdrinier wire-parts are also used in conjunction with secondary head-boxes in the manufacture of linerboard and other grades.

CYLINDER MACHINE. In the case of the basic forming cylinder, significant design modifications include: improved approach-flow systems; restricted and variable vat circles; hollow vacuum and pressure moulds; dry-vat cylinder machines, etc.

FORMERS. A development predicted on the traditional cylinder mould principle is the so-called "formers". Typical examples are the Rotiformer and Stevens Former. These and other formers differ from conventional cylinder vats in the construction of the mould and in their more sophisticated approach-flow stock systems. The latter include multistream and secondary flow boxes, used in the application of several plies formed on one cylinder mould.

DOUBLE WIRE DRAINAGE DEVICES. There is a major disadvantage in the wet-end construction of conventional forming machines of Fourdrinier and cylinder design. This lies in the method by which water is removed from the progressively forming thickened fibre suspension on the machine wire.

With Fourdrinier machines, initially, water leaves the fibre suspension by free drainage. But as the drained fibre mat becomes "thicker", it imposes a disproportionately increasing resistance to drainage of further water retained by the still fluid fibre suspension above it.

In order to increase machine speed, particularly in the manufacture of paperboards, an increase in wire length is inevitable. Also the wet-end part has to be larger and more massive. Similar considerations apply in the manufacture of paperboards on cylinder-type machines.

A method by which water could be drained from both sides of the sheet simultaneously would have considerable advantages. This became increasingly apparent from the growing demand from the packaging industries for paperboards of all types at economic cost. Resistance to drainage on the wire would be considerably less and would be reflected in more compact and less expensive machines. In addition, the mechanism of web formation associated with both Fourdrinier and cylinder machines produces such troubles as sheet two-sidedness and loss of web strength. The concept of double wire drainage is therefore intrinsically appealing. However, the hydrodynamics of double wire drainage impose certain difficulties. Of particular importance is the wire geometry, especially at points of convergence. Unsuitable design causes drainage back flow, which seriously impairs sheet formation.

Typical of double wire drainage machines are the Inverform and Verti-Forma machines. Other variations of the double wire drainage principle exist which more closely resemble cylinder machines.

3.4.1.1 MULTIVAT BOARD MACHINES

Cylinder-vat formation differs basically from Fourdrinier formation, because the cylinder (mould) picks up individual fibres from a stock suspension, in contrast to the Fourdrinier wire, on which fibres are deposited from an inflowing stock suspension from which water is immediately removed by draining. Formation on conventional cylinder-machine vats involves:

1 The whole suspension introduced into the vat participates in sheet formation over a large wire area.
2 Throughout forming, relative movement exists between stock and wire.
3 Owing to speed differentials, half of the fibres deposited on top of the fibrous matt becomes washed off.

Washing-off increases with progressive sheet formation and internal resistance of the matt to backwater flow. Thus, a three phase formation exists:

1 A proportional fibre deposition, with continuous drainage and selective retention.
2 Selective deposition, as suction falls off owing to increasing matt resistance.
3 Pick-up.

Fines content increases continuously in both contraflow and uniflow vats in stage 1 and 2.

CONTRAFLOW VAT (Fig. 3.5). In a conventional contraflow vat, stock enters against the directional rotation of the cylinder. According to Fig. 3.5 the following flow characteristics occur:

1 Incoming stock enters the vat in highly turbulent flow and subsides quickly.
2 It then moves from the inlet side to the immersion zone opposite, where major sheet formation occurs. In this area the suspension is in practically stagnant movement and, thus, is strongly flocculated at the point of initial formation.
3 Adjacent to the moving wire surface, a boundary layer is formed ($\frac{1}{2}$ in thick) in which stock moves at high speed in the same direction as the wire. Because of continued drainage without corresponding fibre deposition, the consistency of this layer rises to a level between the matt and incoming stock.
4 The stream of thickened stock follows the cylinder to the point of emergence, mixes with the incoming stock and is recirculated to the immersion zone. This accounts for the unwanted high consistency at the point of immersion.

5 A turbulent boundary layer is formed between the two different and oppositely moving stock streams, which sets up turbulent secondary currents creating non-uniform flow conditions that leads to variations in substance profile and dry solids content.

Because of (4) above, contraflow formation shows more marked flocculation on the wire side than with uniflow. Good formation only occurs towards the point of deposition of freshly dispersed stock entering the vat.

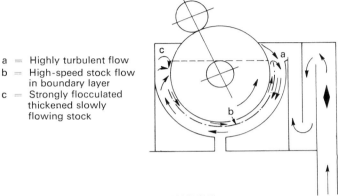

a = Highly turbulent flow
b = High-speed stock flow
    in boundary layer
c = Strongly flocculated
    thickened slowly
    flowing stock

Figure 3.5. CONTRAFLOW CYLINDER MOULD MACHINE

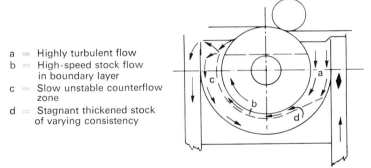

a = Highly turbulent flow
b = High-speed stock flow
    in boundary layer
c = Slow unstable counterflow
    zone
d = Stagnant thickened stock
    of varying consistency

Figure 3.6. UNIFLOW CYLINDER MOULD MACHINE

UNIFLOW VAT (Fig. 3.6). With the uniflow vat, again, there is marked turbulence:

1 At the stock inlet, which quickly subsides as the stock flows downwards towards the vat centre.
2 Immediately following immersion, there takes place a violent initial formation and a major portion of the incoming water is drained away immediately.

At the wire surface, again, a boundary layer is formed at the wire. A relatively large volume of stock is carried to the other side of the vat in this layer. Similar to the contraflow vat, wash-off occurs and results in rise in consistency of the boundary layer. At the point of emergence, the thickened stock separates from the cylinder, but contrary to expectation and previously held views, does not move away at the overflow, but largely reverses direction and passes along the vat walls downwards, where it is finally stopped by incoming stock. In uniflow vats, pick up therefore takes place in the region of returned flow, where stock movement is so slight that the marked flocculation is not surprising. Moreover, long fibres predominate in the vat stock after selective deposition and these are especially prone to flocculation, and are picked up by the web. This is why the uppermost layer in the uniflow vat varies distinctly in flocculation and fines content from the layers below.

3.4.1.2 INTERMITTENT BOARD MACHINE

Mention should be made of the intermittent board machine used in the manufacture of certain speciality end-use boards.

In principle the sheet is couched in the normal manner from a revolving cylinder, but a suction roll can be used instead. It then passes to a press nip, the upper roll of which acts as a "making roll". A progressively thicker sheet can be formed from several layers of fibres which continue to wrap round the roll until the desired board thickness is reached. At this stage a divider releases the sheet from the roll. The sheet is then placed by hand on a lay table behind the machine. The manner of operation allows sheets of varying thicknesses to be obtained.

The sheets are now pressed in the same way as hand-made paperboards. Subsequent drying is carried out by passing the sheets through drying tunnels. Care must be taken to condition the boards before milling, hence the name "millboard".

Milling consists of passing the boards through heavy rollers which have a smoothing and flattening action. This slow semi-automatic process is, therefore, costly and is only used for qualities such as boot and shoe and case boards.

Because the above method of manufacture, in which the sheets of board coming off the machine are removed by hand, is slow, efforts have been directed towards an improved type of machine. There are recorded some 50 patents aimed in this direction. Figure 3.7 shows diagrammatically the results of one notable development for the continuous production of boards. This particular arrangement is available either with a stacking unit for the wet boards; a single sheet flat press unit; or a conventional type of press roll section as illustrated. In the latter case, a stacking frame or a dryer can follow the press section, with a two way sheet cutter.

The method of "dividing" the sheet from the "making roll" is a patented method relying on a process of feeding compressed air through nozzles in a pipe passing across the barrel of the roll, Fig. 3.8.

The alternatives for "handling" as noted, allow, respectively, production of boards of 30–32% dry solids from waste paper up to a grammage of 2,000 g/m^2; 50–55% dry solids up to 2,000 g/m^2; and 40–42% dry solids, up to about 1,000 g/m^2. Output from a 240 cm (95 in) machine, is, respec-

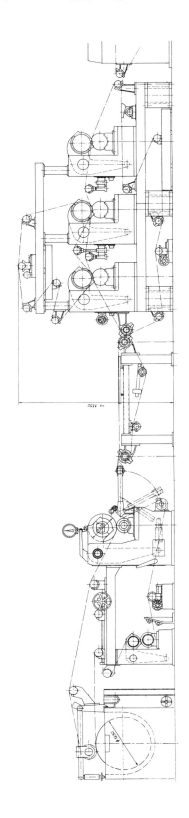

Figure 3.7. INTERMITTENT BOARD MACHINE

Figure 3.8.   INTERMITTENT BOARD MACHINE PRESS SECTION

tively, noted as: 8–12 ton/24 hr; 12–16 ton (both at a machine speed of 20–60 m/min); and 8–10 tons at a speed of 20–45 m/min.

Depending on the type of pulp (usually waste paper), one or two cylinder moulds can be used in uniflow or counterflow arrangement. Carrying tapes transport the sheet from the "making roll" through to the stacking unit or according to the alternative layouts described earlier.

In the case of the stacking frame, wet board sheets are lifted from the transport tape by suction boxes. The sheets are then swivelled through 180° and stacked. The insertion of cloth or metal plates is done by hand.

With the single sheet flat press unit, boards pass under the press at machine speed. It is equipped with a built-in felt press and guidance system. The press runs at a maximum 150 press cycles/hr. Maximum pressure is 35 kp/cm² (498 lb/in²), operating against a rubber membrane and steel plate.

Boards passing to the press roll section do so on a similar arrangement of transport tapes, from which they are conveyed to a press felt ahead of the actual press roll section.

3.4.1.3 MODIFIED APPROACH FLOW VATS

A number of successful attempts have been recorded of modifications to inlet and outlet systems of conventional cylinder vats. Such modifications are aimed at improving inflow arrangements to give closer control over stock flow (fibre velocity pattern) so that inherent tendencies towards fibre alignment or flocculation resulting from conventional (direct) pressure from stock head is minimized.

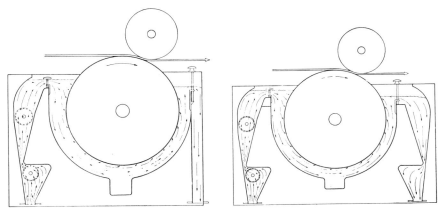

Figure 3.9 (a) and (b).   MODIFIED APPROACH FLOW VATS
The new style inlet (top) can be incorporated in standard counterflow vat design, with beneficial effect on furnish homogeneity and sheet formation.
Combination vat, with new inlet at both sides, allows use of either a counter- or direct-flow vat.

One such attempt, Fig. 3.9, aims at providing a dual purpose contra- or uniflow vat. Claimed with this particular American design (which feeds a 330 cm (134 in) trim board machine) is: overall improvement in formation; upgrading of quality; reduced maintenance and greater ease in cleaning.

3.4.1.4   THE ROTIFORMER

The Rotiformer is a versatile machine incorporating the use of vacuum, gravity and hydraulic pressure for drainage, used in the manufacture of a wide variety and basis weights of paper and boards, e.g., saturating papers, synthetic fibre content papers, cylinder board liners, etc. Speeds range from a few feet per minute up to 175 m/min (500 ft/min), with a potential speed of 350 m/min. Rotiformer formation is generally considered better than that obtained from cylinder vat machines and has the ability to operate at much higher speeds. High dilutions produce better formation and the Rotiformer can handle consistencies as low as 0·02%; particularly important with synthetic fibres; also the vacuum in the forming area picks up very free stocks. High dilutions produce better formation and the Rotiformer that would "roll" in a normal vat permits the use of high freeness stocks.

Dryness of the sheet on leaving will vary with stock and vacuum conditions. The machine is equipped with multiple suction boxes to act on the sheet at various points. Dryness conditions, accordingly, vary from approximately 10% up to as high as 35% solids content, by varying vacuum in the various compartments. This control enables a wide variety of stocks to be used, with production of excellent sheet profiles, and produces good ply bonding in multi-unit operation.

The Rotiformer consists of a cylinder, commonly 118 cm (46 in) diameter, that has no inside supporting structure to obstruct the use of suction boxes. The open-ended cylinder of bronze or stainless steel shell is drilled in similar

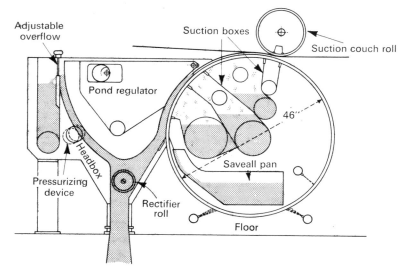

Figure 3.10   PRINCIPLES OF THE ROTIFORMER

fashion to a suction couch roll on a typical paper machine. The outer surface is covered with a wire mesh backing and a facing wire cloth on which a fibre web is formed in the usual manner.

Except that the forming element is a rotating cylinder, Rotiformer has little resemblance to conventional cylinder machines. It is claimed that it combines the best features of both cylinder and Fourdrinier machines. The cylinder does not rotate in a vat of furnish, but uses a headbox and controlled velocity forming area. In this respect it, like the Ultra Former, utilizes some Fourdrinier-type papermaking principles. Suction boxes inside the cylinder shell provide maximum control of forming and de-watering. A patented adjustable pond regulator located within the headbox defines the forming area and controls stock velocity to the wire of the rotating cylinder. This improves the *random* distribution of fibres during formation which considerably reduces the strong machine directional formation characteristics associated with conventional cylinder machines. The incorporation of only one Rotiformer unit in a typical seven vat board machine effectively reduces pronounced MD/CD (machine-/cross-direction) stiffness ratio.

Initial web formation is by free drainage of water through the wire owing to the hydrostatic head of stock. As fibre deposition begins to build up the web on the wire, the correspondingly slower drainage is assisted by the submerged portion of the first vacuum box. This box also serves to hold the sheet in place as the formed web on the wire emerges into the air. The second vacuum box holds formation and prevents stock rollback and any relative movement between the formed web and the cylinder wire surface. It also induces additional drainage.

The stainless steel headbox is provided with an adjustable level overflow dam. It is fitted to the back side of the cylinder so that the forming area covers about 20% of total cylinder area. It is sealed at the edges against the cylinder by air loaded sealing strips and across the machine by an apron lip.

De-watering control of the web is made by adjustment to the variable position suction boxes inside the shell. An air loaded couch or press roll provides final de-watering of the web, prior to leaving the cylinder. Additional press rolls, dandy rolls or lump breaker rolls can be installed on the cylinder face when desired.

3.4.1.5 DRY VAT (RESTRICTED VAT)

Because with conventional vat formation the forming surface is dragged through the suspension longer than is necessary for sheet formation, and because stationary and regular flows are formed in the vat, a vat modification has been made to restrict the forming zone.

The advantages with restricted vats (trough-less or dry vats) are a substantial reduction in wash-off and the elimination of uncontrolled stock flows, which result in improved sheet lookthrough and substance profile.

Stock does not enter the vat over a simple weir, but enters tangentially at relatively high velocity through adjustable slices. The lower slice, through which a greater portion of stock flows, is of primary importance and causes strong circulation and downward flow of stock along the vat wall, where it is deflected as shown in Fig. 3.11. The strong current prevents flocculation. Accumulation of thickened stock near the point of emergence is prevented by the "injector effect" of the upper slice. The thickened fibrous material is continually sucked off and intermixed with incoming stock.

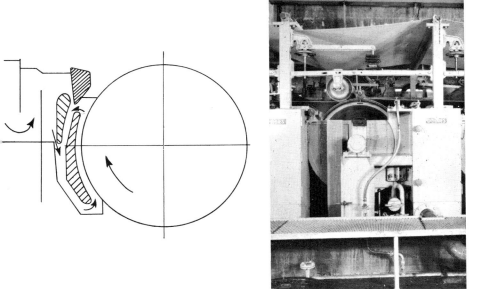

Figure 3.11. DRY VAT CYLINDER MOULD MACHINE

Slice widths are adjustable by slight rotation of the two flaps, which can also be used to control speed of stock circulation, consequently affecting the tensile strength of the sheet. In order to prevent any slight turbulence which may still exist in this design, substance profiles are further improved by the insertion of a flow stabilizer. Many restricted vats are already in operation.

Restricted flow vats are ideal for making multi-ply, heavy board grades at 130 m/min in contrast to cylinder mould machines at 280 m/min. Restricted flow vats substantially improve sheet quality, formation and basis weight profile.

Reportedly, dry vats have reduced weight variation from ± 6–7% obtained with conventional vats to ± 3–4%, a 100% improvement.

Many dry vats are now in use in cylinder board mills, typically in liner positions. It has been the most popular of the new forming devices because of its simplicity, ease of changeover from a conventional vat and low cost. It has been referred to in the US as "the poor man's former" and "an inexpensive steal from everything else."

Principles of dry vat operation employing a "restricted forming mould" are:

1 Formation takes place with well dispersed fibres in a dilute suspension.
2 The washing-off action is reduced or eliminated.
3 White water head differentials in the mould are eliminated, resulting in a uniform head differential for improved formation.
4 Many compressibly resilient materials can be used for the seal. (Low compression set, solvent resistant soft synthetic rubber is preferred.)

Forming capacity is affected by height of the making board over the horizontal seal, and by vacuum in the mould. Ply bond problems occur on boards over 0·030 in–120 lb/MSF. Top commercial speed reported to date is over 166–200 m/min (500 ft/min), with 600 ft/min or over possible. Apparently, in no installation is the dry vat the limiting speed factor.

3.4.1.6 TAMPELLA DRY VAT

A typical and recent dry vat construction, Fig. 3.12, is that of the Tampella dry vat intended for the production of high quality multi-ply paperboard at speeds up to 120 m/min. For higher speeds the makers recommend their suction former.

These dry vats are operating on several board machines currently producing white lined chipboard, folding boxboard, test liner, etc., in basis weights between 200–500 g/m², coated and uncoated. Operational details are given in Table 3.1.

Particular advantages claimed include: speeds from 25–120 m/min; cross-machine basis weight profile variation within $\pm 1\cdot5$–$2\cdot0\%$ with good

Table 3.1. OPERATIONAL DATA FOR TAMPELLA DRY VAT

		Min	Normal	Max
Stock freeness	°SR	30	40–50	75
Stock consistency	%	0·25	0·35–0·50	0·75
Stock flow	l min. m	600	1000–1200	1800
Overflow	l min. m		70–90	
Vacuum in suction slice	mH₂O	0·1	0·2	0·3
Couch roll line pressure	kp/cm		2–3	

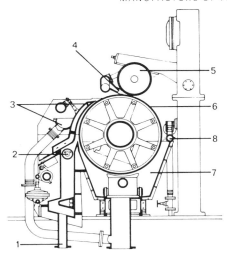

1. Stock inlet
2. Distributor roll
3. Overflow device
4. Suction slice
5. Couch roll
6. Cylinder mould
7. Saveall pan
8. Oscillating shower

Figure 3.12.   TAMPELLA DRY VAT

The dry vat consists of a manifold pipe which divides the flow from the header to four branches entering the inlet chamber. An even flow across the machine is achieved by throttling the flow in the inlet section by means of an adjustable beam running across the entire width of the head box and by changing the direction of the flow. A rotating perforated roll prevents flocculation. This roll has a variable speed drive.

In the sheet formation area the stock flows between the curved top lip assembly and the cylinder mould.

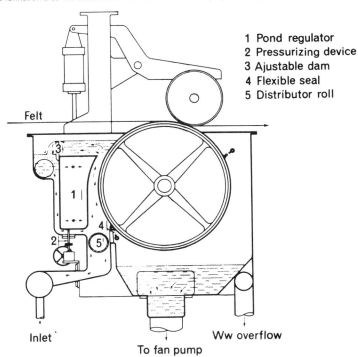

1 Pond regulator
2 Pressurizing device
3 Ajustable dam
4 Flexible seal
5 Distributor roll

Figure 3.13.   ADJUSTABLE DRY VAT CYLINDER MACHINE

Figure 3.14 ADJUSTABLE DRY VAT CYLINDER MACHINE

sheet formation; strength and stiffness ratio between 2·0–2·5: 1; plybond values of 70–130 Scott ($10^3 \times$ lb ft/in^2); basis weight range per vat is 25–100 g/m^2 av, 40–60 g/m^2. The mould is driven by its felt only.

3.4.1.7 ADJUSTABLE DRY VAT CYLINDER MACHINES

A cylinder machine vat design identified as the adjustable dry vat, as described below, is based on the dry vat concept and incorporates features developed by Sandy Hill with its Rotiformer.

The dry vat concept was the result of the board industry's attempt to develop an inexpensive modification of existing counterflow vats, to improve the uniformity and reliability of counterflow operations. The principle is to reduce the forming area of the vat circle by restricting it to the upturning side of the mould and to provide a greater hydrostatic head in the forming area.

In the adjustable dry vat, stock enters the headbox through a multiple manifold inlet. Because stock entering through a bottom inlet flows in the same direction as rotation of the mould, this vat operates as a direct flow vat and thus provides a sheet with improved formation. The increased head produces a denser sheet on the mould, and reduces the tendency for rollback and sloughing without loss of production.

The pond regulator, located in the forming area, can be adjusted to control the stock flow velocity and with it the directionality of the sheet. It is completely submerged under normal operating conditions, with the overflow dam setting the stock level outside the mould. A higher level would mean more moisture into the nip, and vice versa. An overflow over the dam is maintained, and this recirculation carries any thickening stock away from the forming area over the top of the pond regulator and back to the fan pump for redilution and return to the stock line.

A pressurizing device in the headbox below the pond regulator permits control of recirculation and helps keep the approach flow system balanced.

By restricting the passage below the pond regulator with this device and by moving the pond regulator lip towards the mould, a "pressurized headbox" is created. In effect, the fan pump forces the water through the mould and assists the drainage of slow stocks.

Figure 3.15.   ADJUSTABLE DRY VAT SEAL LIP

An exhaust fan connected to the inside of the mould creates a vacuum of 2·5–5 cm of water column for optimum production capacity. Because air evacuation causes continuing drainage beyond the point of emergence from the pond, sloughing is further reduced. Standard type cylinder moulds are used.

A conventional distributor roll, or homogenizer roll, in the throat of the headbox continuously disperses the fibres and minimizes floccing.

The seal lip, Fig. 3.15, often the cause of problems on dry vat conversions, is similar in design to that used successfully for many years on the Rotiformer.

Both the seal lip and the dispersing roll can be easily removed for maintenance by removing a simple plate on the tending side of the vat and sliding each out into the aisle. The dispersing roll may be either a conventional

Figure 3.16(a). CYLINDER FORMATION CHARACTERISTICS
Modified vat formation is smooth and dense compared with conventional vat formation—vats are adjoining on machine.

holey roll or it may be a patented homogenizer roll. The choice is dependent upon the character of fibres and fillers in the slurry.

3.4.1.8 TAMPELLA SUCTION FORMER

This former is designed for production speeds of 150–300 m/min. In particular, cross-machine basis weight variation has been found to be about ±1–1·5% with good sheet formation. Strength and stiffness ratio are between 2·5–3·1:1 even at high speed. Plybond strength falls within the range 70–150 Scott. The machine is depicted in Fig. 3.17. Instrumentation and operation is shown in Fig. 3.18.

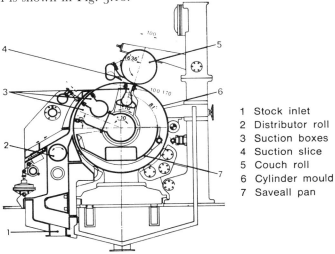

1 Stock inlet
2 Distributor roll
3 Suction boxes
4 Suction slice
5 Couch roll
6 Cylinder mould
7 Saveall pan

Figure 3.17.   TAMPELLA SUCTION FORMER

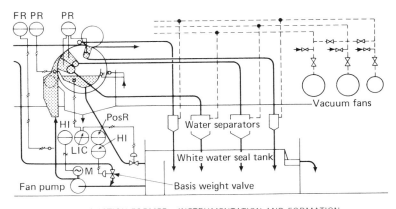

Figure 3.18.   TAMPELLA SUCTION FORMER—INSTRUMENTATION AND FORMATION

Fresh stock is delivered to the suction side of the fan pump through a basis weight regulating valve. Circulation water is taken from the white water seal tank. Initial stock speed to wire ratio is controlled and is usually kept slightly below 1·0. Thus, the rubbing or fibre dragging action which occurs in conventional cylinder moulds is largely eliminated. No overflow is used.

3.4.1.9 VERSA VAT

The Versa Vat is a cylinder board forming device similar in construction to a conventional cylinder vat, but with a superior inlet to insure a uniform dispersion of fibres across the vat and with agitation to promote individual suspension of the fibres. It has the added advantage of being capable of operation as a direct flow vat with better formation and lighter weights, or as a counterflow vat. It has a greater production than a conventional vat. It preceded the adjustable dry vat in development, and is somewhat more expensive.

The Versa Vat, made entirely of stainless steel, has two interconnecting approach chambers, each with a venturi throat and a distributor roll. Stock is accelerated through the venturi, then decelerated in the following expansion chamber. This disrupts fibre flow and prevents floccing. The distributor rolls further disperse and break up the fibres. By these deflocing actions and the even flow velocity it generates, this former corrects the chief causes of streak, eddy currents, and other non-uniform flow conditions common to conventional cylinder mould operations.

Adjustable dams in both ends regulate removal of white water from the mould. An ample crossover maintains uniform removal from both ends of the mould. Single, double or triple wing boards may be provided to control flow into the circle. The cylinder mould features streamlined spiders supported on large diameter shafts turning in anti-friction bearings. The elliptical pattern of the spiders tends to reduce agitation in the mould. The mould deck is made of heavy rods and winding wire to assure rigidity and uniformity of surface.

3.4.1.10 STEVENS FORMER

The Stevens Former, Figs. 3.19 and 3.20, is a single wire "open-top" cylinder board vat forming device whose purpose is to make possible higher speeds and improve formation at these faster speeds while reducing variations in grammage and thickness. The original model, which has been in existence over 10 years had a special totally enclosed cylinder mould for vacuum forming. An external centrifugal blower generated the vacuum, and the sheet was formed under a long cover to control tensile MD/CD ratio and promote uniformity. The new model uses a regular cylinder mould and operates without vacuum. An air doctor is employed after the mould pick up to remove water from the underside of the sheet.

Important features of the new Stevens Former are:

1 *Larger slice forming area.* This allows lower stock consistencies and higher gallonage rates.
2 *Improved header design.* Gives a more uniform distribution of stock across the machine.
3 *Improved rectifier roll arrangement.* Eliminates flocculation and permits simple wash up and clean up.
4 *Simplified mould.* A structurally sound conventional cylinder mould can be used, replacing the extra-heavy earlier moulds.

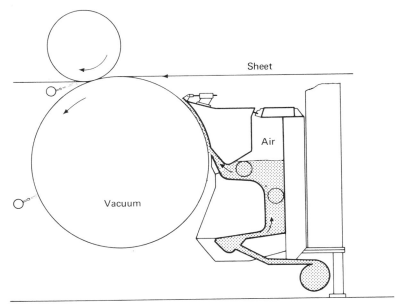

Figure 3.19.   STEVENS FORMER PRINCIPLES

Figure 3.20.   MULTIPLE STEVENS FORMERS IN A CYLINDER BOARD MACHINE

5 *Better cleaning.* Better access around mould facilities cleaning.
6 *Simplified stock system.* The new design uses a very simple stock system. With minimum controls and stock in the system, response to operator adjustment is quick and efficient.
7 The larger slice eliminates the necessity of vacuum systems, seals and controls.

3.4.1.11 HYDRAULIC FORMERS

The hydraulic former is of simple design, Fig. 3.21. Stock enters a cross-machine tapered inlet, passes upwards through multiple tubes into a distribution chamber. Blended stock (from the tubes) now rises through a narrow channel ("hydraulic channel") designed to create small scale turbulence. At the top of the channel, the stock passes through a convergence area and contacts the cylinder mould at an angle of impingement. Some 20–25% of drainage is estimated to take place at this point, the balance of drainage taking place under a curved converging roof. Water drained away falls freely through the base of the mould into a whitewater tank. This eliminates cross machine water gradients in the mould common to conventional vats which discharge from the cylinder ends. It also minimizes water rimming internally.

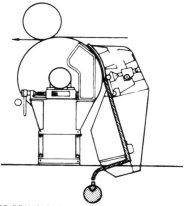

Figure 3.21. HYDRAULIC FORMER PRINCIPLES

These formers use a 106 cm (42 in) cylinder mould and require no more space than a typical 92 cm (36 in) counterflow vat. Each unit should be capable of producing paperboard in thickness 0·3–1·25 mm (0·012–0·048 in) with good coverage and a level sheet profile. Machine to cross machine direction ratio should be in the order of 2:1–2·5:1. In the USA, there are currently three units operating (at time of writing). Experience there is recorded as follows for the three units running out of 8 vats (Stevens?): Taber stiffness MD/CMD 2·7:4·0 (formerly 4·0:5·3). This ratio change is accomplished by a gain in CD stiffness and a loss in MD stiffness, both about the same magnitude. A separation of an individual ply has shown the stiffness ratio to be as low as 2:1 as measured by the tensile modulus elasticity. Within optimum adjustments, formation is superior to the dry vat.

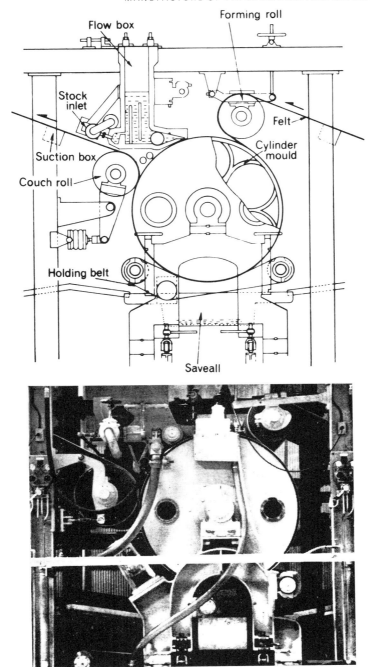

Figure 3.22 (a) and (b).   CONVENTIONAL ULTRA FORMER

Paperboard output by grade (of the installation reported) is mainly combination boxboards—coated and lined carton stock, chipboard and tube stock ranging from 0·4–1 mm (0·016–0·040 in) thickness. After incorporation of hydraulic former units, liner stock used for coated grades was reduced by some 20%. Somewhat smaller reductions were possible on uncoated grades owing to the end-use requirements of these materials for superior opacity and brightness. Best operation is recorded in the freeness range 200–250° CFS for liner stock. Operating speeds of hydraulic formers are possible up to 500–550 ft/min.

3.4.1.12 ULTRA FORMER UNIT

Introduced by the Japanese in 1966, the Ultra Former differs from other forming devices of cylinder and double wire construction. This recent forming device most closely resembles a cylinder machine, but utilizes both cylinder and Fourdrinier forming principles, together with pressure formation and bonding, such as may be found in the Inverform machine. The Ultra Former de-waters and bonds the web between a cylinder face wire and carrier felt, instead of between two wires. Up to eight units can be operated in series to form a complete wet-end in a similar way to the cylinder machine. There are two models, the standard and a high speed version.

Ultra Former utilizes a cylinder mould without a vat. Stock flow in the standard model, Fig. 3.22(a)(b), is from a Fourdrinier-type headbox and slice nozzle arrangement of open or pressure type, directly onto the face of the rotating cylinder. Water drains through the wire, forming the web in conventional manner. The freshly formed web is now bonded to the previously formed web from the last unit carried by a transfer belt. This wraps

Figure 3.23. MULTIPLE ULTRA FORMER VATS IN A BOARD MACHINE

the cylinder mould over 75% of its circumference. A forming roll sandwiches the sheet between felt and cylinder surface.

The high speed model, Fig. 3.24, uses a cylinder wire of Fourdrinier type, supported by the breast roll and cylinder mould. The cylinder mould itself is covered only with a backing wire. Formation box, hydrofoils and suction boxes are arranged in this order and comprise the forming zone. A save-all is provided below the formation zone to receive drained water.

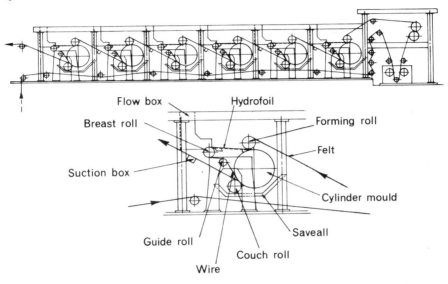

Figure 3.24. HIGH SPEED ULTRA FORMER

Above the cylinder mould is a forming roll (as with the standard model), and below it a suction couch roll. The high speed unit does not, however, have need of the holding belt used in the standard model.

In operation, stock issues from the headbox in similar manner as on a Fourdrinier machine. Thus, the web is already formed before reaching the cylinder mould proper. As the web enters the forming roll, it is bonded together as a single sheet to the web previously formed by the last unit. The combined web is now pressed against the cylinder mould and proceeds on its passage to a couch roll. Here it is sandwiched between a felt and nylon wire, before being conveyed to the wire roll.

Standard Ultra Formers run at about 150/160 m/min (450/480 ft/min), with the high speed machine being capable of up to 350 m/min (1,000 ft/min). Adjustment for change in grade or speed is provided for by an adjustable slice opening. Web formation can be controlled by the headbox in a similar manner to conventional Fourdrinier machines. Stock consistency ranges between 0·2%–1·2% and freeness from 120°–600° CSF.

Important to formation and plybond strength is a small and turbulent puddle. This forms at the nip of the felt and cylinder surface under the forming roll. It re-wets both web surfaces at this point.

An unusual characteristic of the Ultra Former is its water removal ability. The formed sheet on entering the drying machine section contains 10–15% less water than in normal cylinder manufacture. Because drying capacity is often a limiting factor on many board machines (length to machine speed ratio), the lower sheet moisture content offered by Ultra Former has clear economic advantages.

Experience to date indicates that substantial "quality" improvements may be expected from Ultra Former board, in contrast to conventional cylinder made grades and compared with even the latest design of formers predicated on cylinder machines.

In particular, Ultra Former produces boards well suited for gravure printed cartons. Here, important board characteristics include resiliency, uniformity and smoothness. Resiliency is necessary to suck ink out of the gravure print cylinder, and smoothness so that the periphery of each gravure cell is sealed to bring the ink out cleanly.

Particular advantages of the Ultra Former include: high plybond strength; uniformity of sheet structure; smoothness; resiliency (from high bulk); a low MD/CD grain ratio of 2–3.5:1. This ratio affects stiffness and tear strength and is similar to Fourdrinier machine made grades. The grain ratio can be controlled to within limits by adjusting slice or jet velocity relative to cylinder mould speed.

Ultra Former paperboards have 5–10% more bulk compared with cylinder made grades from the same furnish. Ultra Former can make plies in the thickness range 0.41–1.42 mm (0.016–0.055 in) equivalent to 3.5–27 lb MSF.

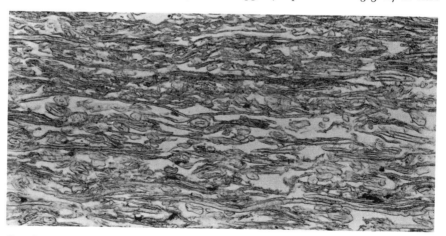

Figure 3.25.   PAPERBOARD FORMATION CHARACTERISTICS

These micrographs illustrate the different sheet formation characteristics of cylinder, Inverform and Ultra Former made paperboards.

Machine direction to cross direction grain ratio affects stiffness and tear strengths in particular. Both are important properties of paperboards.

(a) US made cylinder board, cross section cut parallel to board machine direction—Mag.× 185. Typical MD:CD grain ratio is: 3·6 to 1.
(b) Same as above cut vertical to MD. Mag.× 185.
(c) Inverform board, cross section. Mag.× 125. MD: CD 2·7 to 3.
(d) Ultra Former cross section cut vertical to MD. Mag.× 125. MD: CD: 2 to 3·8 to 1.

It can make lower weights and thicknesses than cylinder machines and economically make higher weights and calipers than Fourdrinier or Inverform machines.

Operational experience to date has shown it is much easier to make wide thickness changes without losing the sheet. Changes from 0·5 to 1–1·5 mm (0·020–0·058 in) can be made without any problem and with no blows or drop-offs, and usually without any wet-end breaks. In addition, such changes can be made more rapidly. For instance, on a cylinder machine it might take 1½ to 2 hours in changing over before the operation levels out on the new grade. With the Ultra Former, the complete change can usually be made in less than half an hour.

3.4.1.13 COMBINATION BOARD MACHINES

Certainly the most common "combination board machines" in operation today still embody Fourdrinier and combined vat operations. This combination makes possible a variety of forming arrangements. They range on the one hand, from a simple Fourdrinier wet-end in combination with three or more—usually four to six—cylinder vats, which are commonly both contraflow and uniflow type to more sophisticated arrangements of one or two Fourdrinier wire sections in combination with cylinder forming devices that can well include conventional contra- and uniflow, cylinder machines running next to or in conjunction with other cylinder-type forming devices including Rotiformer, Ultra Former, etc.

Combination machines such as described are used in the manufacture of a wide range of folding carton grades, and speciality paperboard and board grades.

Machines of this type are particularly common throughout Europe, many of which are relatively complicated in design and construction. Shown in Fig. 3.26 is a combination board machine incorporating a number of interesting features. This type of machine arrangement can be used for making standard folding carton grades in a wide range of thicknesses; fibre furnish components for the different liners; strength specification; surface coating,

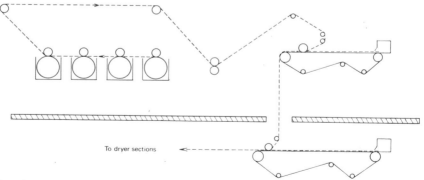

Figure 3.26. "COMBINATION" BOARD MACHINE
Board machine with two Fourdriniers. Fourdrinier wires are on two levels with four cylinder vats.

Figure 3.27. SECOND FOURDRINIER WIRE
Machine direction is from right to left. This wire makes the top liner, which meets the other five layers coming from above.

Figure 3.28. FOURDRINIER MAKING SUB-LINER
Seen here is the Fourdrinier in the upper right corner of Fig. 3.26. The web from above joins onto the sub-liner.

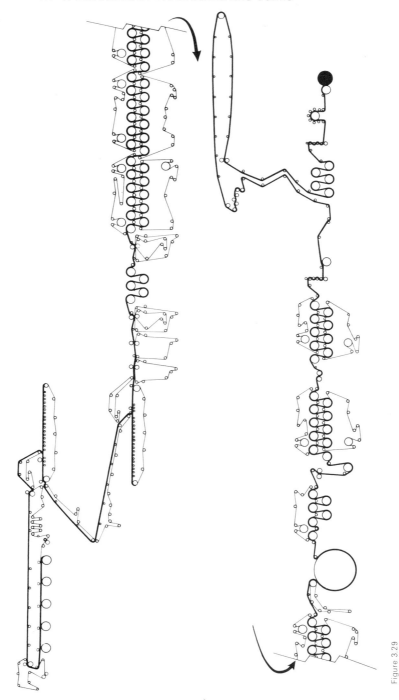

Figure 3.29

Because of process requirements and to save space, this machine is built on two levels. Formation of the top liner takes place on a Fourdrinier wire in conventional manner. Formation of the underliner and filler takes place on five Tampella suction formers, all located on the elevated floor. The bottom liner Fourdrinier is on the main floor. The "combined" web passes through several presses (the fourth press is placed in a hot press position), all equipped with fabric wires, into the dryers, round an MG cylinder in inverted position for easy accessibility and simple web threading, into the after-dryers, through two horizontal size presses, into six roll calender, then passes through a metering bar pre-coater and an air-knife wet-on-wet coating arrangement located on the elevated floor: back down to the lower floor level through further dryers, another six roll calender, and a brush polishing unit before being wound into a mill roll.

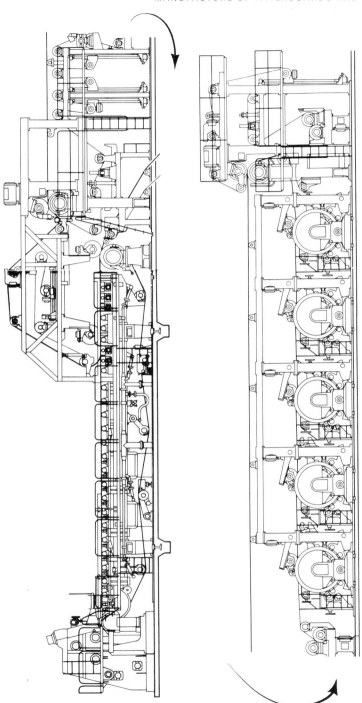

Figure 3.30.   DIAGRAMMATIC LAYOUT OF TOP LEVEL FOURDRINIER AND 5-VAT CYLINDER SECTION MAKING FILLER PLYS AND UNDERLINER

E

Figure 3.31.   The Fourdrinier wire-part looking towards the cylinder section. The web formed by the suction formers is carried by pick up and transfer felts onto the Fourdrinier where it is couched together with the top liner. Fourdrinier wire section and headboxes are air-cushioned.

Figure 3.32.   THE BOTTOM LINER FOURDRINIER
Positioned on the main left floor the web from the upper floor is brought to the lower Fourdrinier by transfer felts—or it can pass straight to the first press.

Figure 3.33. PICTURE SHOWS THE ARRANGEMENT FACING TOWARDS THE WET END

Clearly to be seen is the top sheet (from the top wire) travelling downwards towards the bottom Fourdrinier wire part of the headbox which is situated under the transfer felt at far right. The control panel is seen in the foreground, to the left of which is the suction couch and beginning of the press section.

Figure 3.32: the same arrangement is viewed looking towards the dry end of the machine. Nominal output is 250 tons day of white lined chipboard and test liner within the range 160–500 g/m² (26 lb MSF). Maximum speed is 300 m/min (1000 ft/min).

Figure 3.34. TENDING SIDE OF SUCTION FORMERS

Board suction formers ahead of the Fourdrinier wire that forms the top liner on the elevated floor. Each former has its own control panels.

and so on. Variations on this type of machine design include two Yankee (MG) cylinders between pre- and after-drier cylinders of normal 5 ft diameter, different coating arrangements including bar coating (for pre-coating) and airknife (for top coating), etc.

In Fig. 3.27 the top liner formed on the second Fourdrinier wire (in Fig. 3.26) is shown at its meeting point with the other five layers coming from above. Figure 3.28 shows a view of the Fourdrinier making the sub-liner. The web from above joins the sub-liner at this point.

A number of other unusual and interesting and sophisticated "combination" arrangements exist, all of which are claimed to have certain merits by their developers. Typical of modern arrangements are the diagrammatic illustrations reproduced in Figs. 3.36 to 3.41 and Figs. 3.30 to 3.35.

3.4.1.14 INVERFORM MACHINE

The Inverform machine concept was developed with the object of providing a new method for the manufacture of single and multi-ply sheets at high speeds.

It was owing to difficulty experienced in the downward (conventional) removal of water through several layers of board at higher machine speeds of around 150–166 m/min (450–500 ft/min) and in the thicker substances that attention was focused on a method of upward removal of water—the basic principle underlying the Inverform process.

This technique of manufacture is ideally applied to heavy papers and boards. It allows for both upward and downward drainage for the first layer of fibres, followed by upward removal of water for any number of succeeding layers, without the necessity for drainage through the previously deposited layers.

Inverform is a means of applying pressure to a turbulent layer of pulp slurry for a very short period of time during the entry of the slurry to the in-running nip between the headbox and forming roll, without deformation or crushing of the sheet and with upward removal of water. Figures 3.42(a) and 3.42(b) show the elementary principle of the Inverform unit. Stock flows on to the bottom wire immediately before an in-running nip created by the top wire passing round a large diameter cellular roll, known as the forming roll. The bottom wire is supported under the forming roll by large diameter table rolls and the two wires, with stock sandwiched in between, pass into the auto slice. This is a stiff bevelled scraper blade pressed lightly against the inside top wire. Water forced upwards through the top wire is swept up the sloping blade into the tray and then returned to the machine pit. In the case of a single ply board or the first layer of a multi-ply, a quantity of water naturally passes downwards but, after the first ply has been put on to the bottom wire, very little water from the following plies can pass downwards and must therefore be extracted upwards. At speeds below 270 m/min (800 ft/min) it is necessary to assist water to travel up the sloping blade of the auto slice. Further water is removed after the auto slice by inverted suction boxes, conventional flat boxes being used in addition during the first single ply operation. (Vacuum is between 2–3.5 in Hg.) Final de-watering is

Figure 3.35. BOARD MACHINE VIEWED FROM THE REEL UP END

Here viewed from the reel up end, the brush polishing unit for glazing is clearly seen, behind this are two six-roll calenders of open-face type. The first calender has a crown controlled bottom roll.

Also to be seen (middle of picture) is the coated web coming down from the coating installation positioned on the elevated floor.

achieved by a small press roll (the bottom roll housed in a suction box and the top rubber covered roll fitted with a suction slice) followed by a suction couch roll. The auto slice consists of a resin bonded laminated blade with stainless steel trays, the slice being adjustable.

The main advantages of the Inverform process are:

1 Greatly increased speeds.
2 Improved formation.
3 Better substance profile.
4 Improved ply adhesion (controllable).
5 Increased bulk.
6 Higher stock consistencies can be employed. For example, short fibred stock from $1\cdot3-1\cdot8\%$; long fibred stock from $0\cdot7-1\cdot2\%$.
7 A wide range of freeness can be used without a reduction in speed, e.g., from $700°$ to $50°$ CSF.

A considerable number of Inverform board machines are now installed around the world. Inverform is used in the manufacture of a wide range of paperboards, e.g., kraftliner, jute liner, fluting medium, solid foodboard and boxboard grades, etc.

INVERFORM OPERATION. Board mill experience indicates that Inverform formation is best at low stock consistencies—headbox $0\cdot5-0\cdot8\%$ range. Higher consistency is best operated in intermediary headboxes, as in the

Fourdrinier paper machine

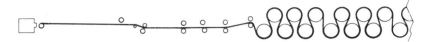

Fourdrinier and multi-cylinder combination machine

Fourdrinier and 3 layer combination machine

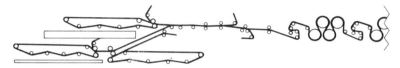

Fourdrinier and TK former combination machine

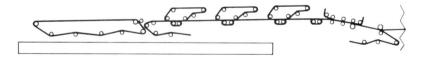

Ultra former paper machine

Figures 3.36—41   "COMBINATION" BOARD MACHINE ARRANGEMENTS

The above illustrations provide a pictorial feature of the important common combined board machine arrangements in operation today.

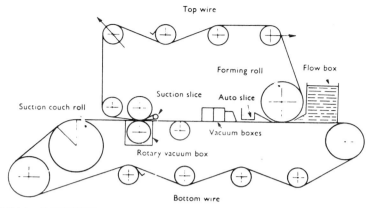

Figure 3.42(a). ELEMENTARY ARRANGEMENT OF AN INVERFORM UNIT

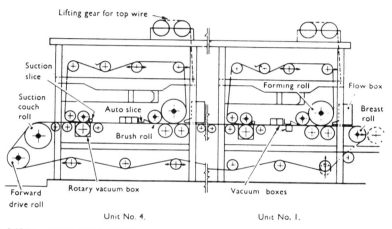

Figure 3.42(b). FOUR-UNIT INVERFORM (MIDDLE STATIONS OMITTED)

manufacture of middle plies in boxboard grades, which need to be heavier than the two outer plies.

Stock velocity is a critical variable affecting board quality. Good results have been reported when running wire speed and stock velocity close to each other.

In the manufacture of boxboard grades in Europe, a freeness of 500–550°CSF appears suitable and is in keeping with American practice. Normal air dry moisture content for Inverform board is 6·5–7%.

Miscellaneous operating factors include:

1 The size of the small back flow pond in the Inverform's forming roll nip is important. If the pond is too large, the turbulent activity is considerably reduced and air is drawn into the nip.

2 Operation of the forming roll and auto slice are important. Overloading will force rejection of stock causing excessive flow of water laterally in

the respective nips which results in crushing of the sheet. Similarly, an excessive flow of stock to the forming roll nip gives rise to a very large pond and can have deleterious effects on formation.

3 The immobilized sheet between the two wires is extremely sensitive to relative movement of the wires. Thus serious damage results from the wire velocities not being closely synchronized, or from a slack top wire between forming roll and auto slice.

4 Formation appears to be improved by increased machine speed. At speeds below 90–100 m/min (290–330 ft/min) it is difficult to obtain good formation.

5 Tensile and stiffness ratios are controlled predominantly by the stock-to-wire velocity ratio. Roughly, the MD:CD ratio falls between ratios obtained by Fourdrinier and counterflow cylinder operations.

6 When stock velocity exceeds wire velocity, it has been found formation degenerates rapidly.

7 Symmetry of the Inverform sheet, with regard to two sidedness and surface fibre orientation, is extremely good. The sheet is often referred to as being "square" in terms of its formation and strength properties. This is in contrast to Fourdrinier made grades where the machine to cross direction ratio is usually high.

8 Moisture content of the sheet must be controlled from one Inverform unit to the next in a multi-unit Inverform machine. If, for example, the solids are too low, a water crush can be experienced. Conversely, if the solids go too high, ply-bonding efficiency diminishes rapidly.

9 Regarding the basis weight capabilities of the Inverform, it has been the experience of one mill that a maximum of 210 g/m² can be applied and formed at the first station, and then 100 g/m² on each side of the (usually four) remaining stations. A minimum substance in the region of 11 g/m² each ply in a 3-ply web has been successfully produced.

TOP LINER APPLIED AT THE LAST INVERFORM STATION. A particular advantage in Inverform operation is that the top board liner can be applied at the last station or stations. This is in so-called "backwards" fashion to early Inverform board making practice, where the top liner was invariably applied at the beginning. It is probable that this discovery originated at a Scottish mill.

The main benefits of applying the liner thus, are:

1 It is the way in which board is formed on other board machines.

2 Full water removal capacity of the first Inverform station can be used because full vacuum on a single web layer may be applied without disturbing sheet formation. This results in a denser sheet and makes full use of less costly, secondary fibre stock for the back liner.

3 A reserve press in the press section (necessary with "non-backward" operation Inverforms) is not needed, i.e., straight through presses are therefore suitable.

4 Because the top liner does not assume the rôle of the "foundation" ply, a lighter layer of the more expensive "pure" cellulose pulp component

can be applied without giving rise to poor formation, poor ply bonding or loss of covering power over the low colour backing plies.

3.4.1.15 VERTI-FORMA

The principle of the Verti-Forma arrangement is a departure from conventional approaches to formation, and most resembles twin wire machines in concept.

The underlying principle of this development was to produce a sheet of paper with identical characteristics on both surfaces, currently impossible to produce on conventional Fourdrinier or cylinder machine equipment.

The basic configuration (Fig. 3.43) consists of a twin wire forming device operating in a vertical plane, and involves two symmetrically arranged forming wires, plus stretch and guide rolls, showers and save-all pans. The wires pass around metering rolls, Fig. 3.44 (which serve the dual function of the slice and breast roll on a conventional machine), and the driven suction rolls and wire drive rolls. Metering and drive rolls are horizontally adjustable. The metering roll-headbox assembly is vertically adjustable to permit a variable control length of the forming zone over a considerable range.

Suction boxes and/or forming boards, deflectors or scrapers are adjustably mounted and arranged on both sides of the wire, so that symmetrical drainage can take place. After the suction boxes, both wires part. The web follows one of the wires and passes over a roll that resembles a suction couch, the sheet being transferred at this point. Suction transfer and the pick-up

Figure 3.43. VERTI-FORMA ARRANGEMENT

Off-set couch rolls (top) at bottom of forming zone are of plain design for the backing wire (right) and suction design for the carrying wire (left). Formation is accomplished within a four foot vertical area between the breast roll centre line and the leading edge of the suction-holding box.

Figure 3.44.   VERTI-FORMA HEADBOX SLICE
Viewed from machine backside is the headbox slice, breast rolls, and tapering gap between the two forming wires.

arrangement are especially designed to provide a tangential take-off from the wire. This substantially minimizes sheet stresses during transfer to the pick-up felt.

The Verti-Former in a commercial sense is still being developed. At the time of writing its first installation (in Canada) is specializing successfully in the production of groundwood grades. The first machine to produce fluting medium is reported to be operating in Japan at 1,800 ft/min.

3.4.1.16 PAPRIFORMER MACHINE

The Papriformer is a compact web former developed by the Pulp and Paper Research Institute of Canada. Stock is injected between two forming screens. These firstly partly wrap a forming roll on which the stock is

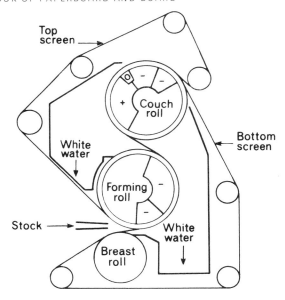

Figure 3.45. PAPRIFORMER MACHINE

partly de-watered by drainage through the screens. The screens then partly wrap a couch roll as can be seen from Fig. 3.45.

At the time of writing the machine is still in its early commercial development stages. For this reason description of it here is short.

The Papriformer was designed in order to overcome some of the web forming limitations and shortcomings of the Fourdrinier machine, and in consequence its inherent limitations to productive capacity. This it appears to have done.

In very broad terms, basis weights in the 127–160 g/m² range would seem practical. A 127 g/in² (0·009 in) fluting medium is recorded as having been made without operating difficulty.

3.4.1.17 MULTI-FORMER

The high speed Multi-former is a recently announced development that incorporates several basic improvements in cylinder machine design to produce multiple-ply paperboards at speeds to 300 m/min (1,000 ft/min) with controlled CD/MD strength ratios. The machine cylinders are located in a stair-stepped arrangement to yield maximum drainage and optimum handling of whitewater, Fig. 3.46. The arrangement provides a straight sheet path. The design additionally reduces the horizontal length of the machine. Since transfer is at the bottom of the cylinders, the felt or wire becomes a carrier, rather than a pick-up belt, thus eliminating any possibility of drop-offs.

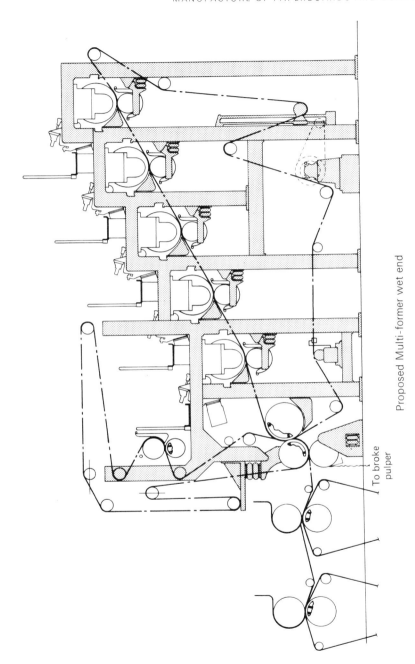

Proposed Multi-former wet end

To broke
pulper

Figure 3.46.   PROPOSED MULTI-FORMER WET END

FORMATION CONTROLLED BY HEADBOXES. In the Multi-former, a slurry is laid on each cylinder near the top, in the direction of cylinder rotation. The slurry is de-watered and a ply is removed at the bottom of the cylinder on the felt or wire belt. As the belt passes beneath each successive cylinder, a new ply is deposited on top of the ply or plies already formed.

Headbox and slice are pressurized. High velocities are maintained in the headbox channels to prevent flocculation and to assure random orientation of fibres.

Cylinders are suction type; a drilled shell rotates around a suction box. Each cylinder applies a forming, drainage, holding and transfer pressure to the slurry, to form a single damp ply on the cylinder surface by the time it rotates to the felt. Nip pressure of the couch roll at the felt transfer point further dries the ply.

Whitewater removed by the suction roll is drained away by gravity in the direction of cylinder rotation. The drainage pan lip begins immediately following the point of ply transfer, and water is centrifugally thrown off into the pan. This feature is in marked contrast with designs that trap drainage between the ply and the cylinder. As a result, a drier ply is produced. Also it is impossible for the ply to wrap the cylinder.

With less pressing equipment at the machine wet-end than in conventional installations, the Multi-former still furnishes a drier sheet to the dryer section.

In a pilot installation of the Multi-former in a mill, two ply paperboard sheets have been produced at speeds of 244 m/min (800 ft/min). Design capability of the installation is 300 m/min (1,000 ft/min).

Squareness of the finished sheet can be controlled by headbox slice positioning. Ratios of 1–1.5:1 are readily obtained, as contrasted to the 4:1 ratios commonly experienced in cylinder machine production.

By a combination of Fourdinier-type slice formation with vacuum cylinders, high unit ply weights are obtainable. This permits production of average weights of lined boxboard on a total of five units, as shown in the reproduced wet-end diagram. Overall height of a typical wet-end will be approximately 6 m (20 feet).

The Multi-former claims important economic advantages: high quality, coatable board can be manufactured from reclaimed fibres and white linen boards can be produced with minimum weights of top liner furnish.

3.5 board machine press section

The primary objective of the press section of a board machine (whether a standard Fourdrinier machine or a cylinder-type machine) is to remove as much water as possible from the wet web as it leaves the forming wire and before it enters the drying section.

The most radical way to increase paper dryness in a press is through greater sheet compression. However, the sheet at this stage is in a very plastic state. It is readily subject to "deformation" as a result of strains and stresses. Pressure should thus always be applied gradually at the various presses, in order to allow water held in the fibres by capillary attraction to be released

Figure 3.47. TYPICAL INVERFORM BOARD MACHINE PRESS SECTION

slowly. The action of pressing increases paperboard strength and its apparent specific gravity. However, undue pressure or disturbance in the sheet through stretching at this stage will produce lower dry sheet strength values.

3.5.1 *Sheet consolidation*

The wet web as it passes through a press nip is subject to increasing and decreasing pressure. Pressure gradients are established which cause water to flow, some of which leaves the sheet to be taken up by the wet felt, or in the case of fabric presses by the fabric. As water leaves, the fibre mass is compacted causing more intimate contact between fibres, thus providing a better opportunity for the development of intra- and inter-fibre bonding during drying. Broadly speaking, wet pressing has the same kind of effects on dry sheet properties as typical refining. Wet pressing effects are, however, dependent on beating degree and under certain conditions fibre bonding appears not to be increased by wet pressing. Wet pressing depends on the degree of elastic resistance and plastic conformability of the fibres which determines the "spring-back" reaction of the fibrous web on exit from the press nip, bearing in mind that fibre-to-fibre bonds are formed over exceedingly small distances (see section 2.4.1.1). Nevertheless, wet pressing under certain conditions greatly augments the conditions needed for satisfactory development of dry sheet characteristics during drying.

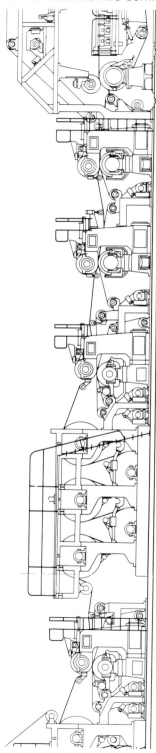

Figure 3.48(a)   BOARD MACHINE PRESS SECTION—DIAGRAMMATIC

Figure 3.48(b)   BOARD MACHINE PRESS SECTION

3.5.2 *Removal of water*

The theory of the mechanism of water removal in the nip of a suction press involves two phases. The first phase concerns an initial compression of the paper and felt during entry into the roll nip. The usual explanation of water removal has previously been attributed to this phase, i.e., during entry into the nip the felt and web are compressed, so that water is taken up from the web by the felt and then removed from the felt, the process being completed before reaching the midway point of the nip.

However, the now accepted interpretation is that in fact, water removal from the web by the felt actually takes place at the point of felt recovery in the outgoing side of the nip. Water removal from the felt, then, actually takes place during its ingoing passage to the nip. As the felt is saturated, water is expressed along the line of least resistance, i.e., either backwards through the felt in the nip of a plain press and out of the nip, or into the holes of a suction press.

3.5.3 *Different press types*

There are a number of different presses available. They include traditional suction presses, fabric presses, vented nip presses, etc.

Of the more recent press designs the Venta-nip press in particular is remarkably simple and efficient.

3.5.3.1 FABRIC PRESS

The principle of the fabric press, see Fig. 3.49, is to prepare a non-compressible space in the press nip for the transport of water pressed out of

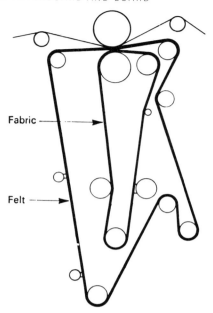

Figure 3.49.   FABRIC PRESS ARRANGEMENT

the paper web and felt. The latest theories about the operation are that total pressure is used for compressing paper and felt and also for building up hydraulic pressure, i.e., bringing about a water flow. With a wire in the nip, resistance to the flow of water is less and more pressure is consequently available for compression of the felt. The total nip pressure is just as great, whether a wire is under the felt or not, although the maximum point and distribution of the pressure can vary.

In a plain press, resistance to the flow of water is greater and the felt is therefore compressed to a lesser degree. Smaller amounts of water leave the felt and flow instead in a lengthwise direction. By this means a higher hydraulic pressure is obtained. With a wire in the press the water, however, disappears quickly in the cavities of the wire and the hydraulic pressure sinks. The felt should be very permeable and compressible. The wire should have low compressibility, large pore volume and a close surface to prevent the felt from filling the voids, resulting in re-wetting of the web. When paper, felt and wire leave the nip, the water is removed from the wire cavities, and the felt is separated from the paper web to prevent re-wetting. The wire is emptied by the help of a suction box, or is allowed to convey its water content to the bottom press roll. which is kept dry with the help of a doctor blade. The problem of re-wetting is more acute with slow machines running wet stocks, or heavy substance grades. Advantages of a fabric press are:

1   Drier sheet content at higher speeds, at a given pressure, e.g., a moisture content of 34–35% for sack kraft, compared with 30% on a plain press.

2 Increase in production because of (1); or a 10–15% saving in steam consumption during drying.

3 Better retention of fillers through more uniform moisture profile across the sheet.

4 Elimination of "shadow" marking by the action of earlier suction press.

5 Because of higher pressure, sheet surface is smoother.

The fabric press, like a normal plain press, is very dependent on the dry content of the ingoing web. The press arrangement depends on machine speed and can be designed for all speeds, providing the wire and felt are given a more horizontal run through the nip. At high speeds, the wire can wrap the roll even more without any difficulty. Positioning of the top roll is an important factor.

A fabric press may be run in first, second and third press positions and as a reversing press. In third press position the sheet dry solids content has been increased by 4%, by easing the second press and allowing a wetter sheet to pass forward. Also this results in a reduction in "crushing". Position of the felt and wire in relation to press arrangement is of the greatest importance.

3.5.3.2 SHRINK FABRIC PRESS

The shrink fabric press, Fig. 3.50, is a later simplification of the fabric press in which the wire is shrunk tightly on the bottom press roll and fastened at the ends. The shrink fabric can be fitted on solid and suction type presses and many have been supplied in Europe.

A fabric press may be run: in first, second and third press positions and as a press, probably because more water is carried out of the nip (less centrifugal force) and is removed more efficiently by the suction box.

The shrink fabric press, Fig. 3.50, is a later simplification of the fabric presses and gives mainly the same advantage as the fabric press, namely

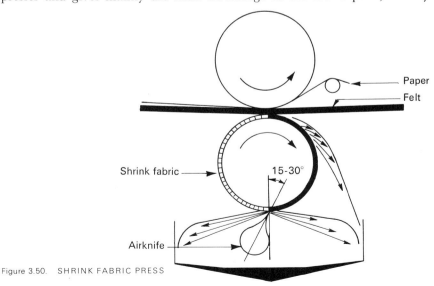

Figure 3.50.   SHRINK FABRIC PRESS

higher web dryness, because a higher pressure can be used without crushing the sheet. The felts can also be run longer, without any detrimental effect to the quality or dryness of the paper.

The most important function of the fabric is to provide for an incompressible space in the press nip; this function is filled equally well by a shrink fabric or by a free fabric.

In the press nip of a fabric press and a shrink fabric press, water can pass straight through the felt. Since the hydraulic resistance of the felt is very low in this direction, more of the total pressure can be utilized for compression. The opposite conditions apply in a plain press.

When the paper web is crushed in a plain press nip, the resistance to the flow of water in the plane of the sheet is lower than the hydraulic resistance against the water flow into the felt. This condition rarely occurs in a fabric press nip. Plugging of the felt affects mainly the hydraulic resistance in the plane of the felt. Since no flow is needed in this direction in a fabric press, felt plugging has very little effect on the operation of the fabric press and shrink fabric press.

The most radical way to increase paper dryness in a press is through greater sheet compression. Factors limiting this in solid (plain) and suction presses are crushing of the sheet, plugging of the felt and mechanical strength of suction roll sheet. None of these factors limits the pressure in a fabric or shrink fabric press and consequently pressure can be raised substantially, e.g., 123 kg/cm (700 lb/linear in) for a first press.

WATER REMOVAL FROM FABRIC PRESSES. In a free fabric press water removal is by means of a doctor against the bottom press roll and a suction box against the felt.

With a shrink fabric press there are three alternatives for removing water:

1 By means of an airknife.
2 Water pressed out through the fabric on the ingoing side of the press nip.
3 Water removal from the press felt through a suction box or in a separate press.

1. *Airknife*

At press speeds over 560 m/min (1,600 ft/min) centrifugal force throws a substantial amount of water from the fabric covered roll. Providing the relative amount of water is small – and always at low speeds – it can be blown away from the fabric by high velocity air, directed through an air jet at a 15° angle to the roll.

2. *Pressure*

If nothing is done to remove water from the felt and fabric before they return to the nip, a hydraulic pressure builds up in the fabric in the first part of the nip and the water is pressed out through the fabric in an opposite direction to its travel. Although the shrink fabric press used in this way functions similarly to the solid (plain) press, there are some important differences. The hydraulic resistance in the felt is very much lower in the shrink fabric press with less risk of crushing the sheet. Furthermore, a hydraulic pressure is built up in the fabric and presses out the water between the felt and fabric covered roll. Because of this pressure, water can leave the system even at a machine speed above 350 m/min (1,000 ft/min) the water cascading out below the felt in the opposite direction to its travel.

3. *Suction box*

The third method of removing water is to de-water the felt by means of a suction box, before it returns to the nip. In a fabric press the felt runs wetter than in a suction or solid press, because the felt reabsorbs much water from the fabric.

3.5.4 *Venta-nip press*

The Venta-nip press, Fig. 3.51, of fairly recent design is remarkably simple. It consists of a normal hard rubber covered roll with grooves around its circumference and all the way across its face. These grooves are cut 2·5 mm

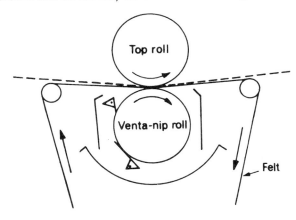

Figure 3.51. VENTA-NIP PRESS ARRANGEMENT

deep and 0·5 mm wide. This specially grooved roll vents both water and air from the nip and provides a press which can replace the complicated and expensive procedure of drilled suction rolls.

With a Venta-nip installation, water can pass straight through the felt into the grooved roll where it is carried away, venting the back side of the felt and eliminating the re-wetting of the web on exit from the nip. Slight wrapping of the felt on the top plain roll, both on entry and exit of the nip, largely prevents re-wetting of the felt and provides for complete separation of water from the sheet and felt.

Positioning of the grooves is such that at no point on the face is the distance greater than *ca.* 1·25 mm (0·050 in) from a vent (the order of the compressed thickness of the felt). By so venting the pressing roll surface, it is essentially impossible to develop a pressure gradient in the plane of the felt and so sheet crushing is greatly reduced or eliminated. The grooved roll effectively vents

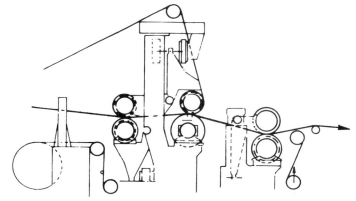

Figure 3.52.   CYLINDER MACHINE VENTA-NIP PRESS ARRANGEMENT

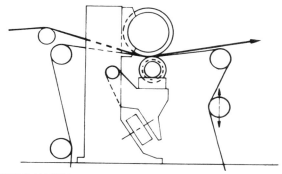

Figure 3.53.   CYLINDER MACHINE CONTROLLED CROWN VENTA-NIP PRESS ARRANGEMENT

the back side of the felt at the high pressure point of the nip and prevents reabsorption of expressed water by the felt.

A particularly satisfactory press section arrangement for multi-ply board machines might include an arrangement shown in Fig. 3.52. This would consist of two primary presses, the first having opposed Venta-nip rolls, the second having a suction bottom roll and Venta-nip top roll (after which the top felt returns) followed by two or three Venta-nip main presses. The first and second presses could be typically loaded up to 31–45 kg/cm (175–250 lb/linear inch). The third press could be loaded to 53 kg/cm (300 lb/linear inch), with the last press at 70 kg/cm (400 lb/linear in).

3.5.5 *UNI-press*

The UNI-press of KMW Co design and manufacture is a latecomer and is one of the most significant press developments in modern papermaking machine design. It is a pick-up press, universally applicable in principle to all grades of paper and paperboard.

This press utilizes the pick-up arrangement as a first press suction roll. The paper web is transferred onto the felt by vacuum, throughout its travel from pick-up point to press nip. No open draw (unsupported sheet transfer) is applied until the web has passed through the press nip, and its dryness and strength are of the same order as is normally obtained after two conventional suction presses.

Positive transfer of the sheet is ensured at all basis weights and machine speeds, as opposed to conventional pick-up press arrangements. The transfer felt can be run dry into the press nip, permitting higher nip pressures without fear of sheet crushing.

In paperboard manufacture, UNI-presses are running on machines manufacturing kraftliner, and fluting medium, Fig. 3.54, respectively at speeds of 600 m/min and 750 m/min in basis weights each of 100–250 g/m² and 100–130 g/m². An important practical advantage is that there is no risk of web breakage, even when running sheets of low web strength at high speeds. Heavy board of basis weight 3,000 g/m² has been run through a UNI-press at a speed of 20 m/min.

The linear pressure that can be applied without the risk of crushing is higher in a UNI-press than in any other kind of first press. The reason for this is that the felt can be run drier on the machine, as the sheet is sucked against the felt and held in position by a vacuum. The dry felt has a high capacity for absorbing water. These presses are today designed for a linear pressure of about 80 kg/cm (450 lb/linear inch). Consequently paper web dryness is

Figure 3.54.   UNI-PRESS INSTALLED ON A MACHINE MAKING FLUTING
This type of press allows "closed" transfer of the sheet from the forming wire to press section and makes for a stronger sheet than is produced by running with an open draw.

higher than is normally obtained beyond two conventional suction presses.

An advantage of a UNI-press in the manufacture of corrugating medium (although this applies equally to all other paper and paperboard grades) is that the "closed" transfer of the sheet from wire to press provides a stronger paper than may be produced by open transfer. At the first open draw after a UNI-press the web dryness is 28–37%. Dimensional changes will be considerably less than for an open transfer. Owing to the UNI-press design there is no risk of structural changes created in the sheet due to crushing. This is true for all normal grades.

A particularly advanced and efficient press arrangement is catered for by a combination of the UNI-press and a fabric press, Fig. 3.55. The fabric press then acts as a second press. It uses two solid press rolls with a fabric wire running through the nip between felt and roll. Water pressed out of the sheet passes straight through the felt and into the voids in the wire. Such an arrangements. The combination of a UNI-press and fabric press can be drier sheet. A wider choice of felt eliminates the risk of "marking" and gives paper and paperboard a better finish. Higher linear pressures can be used and heavier squeeze rolls can be fitted compared with other types of press arrangements. The combination of a UNI-press and fabric press can be

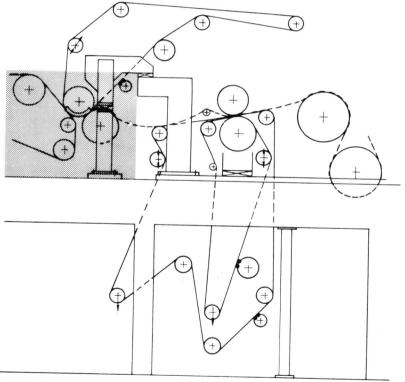

Figure 3.55 UNI-PRESS AND FABRIC PRESS
An advanced and particularly effective press arrangement is catered for by a combination of the UNI-press and a fabric press. UNI-press is shaded area.

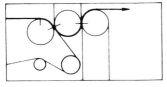

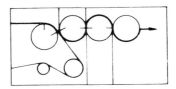

Figure 3.56. DOUBLE-FELTED UNI-PRESS
A pick-up press for paperboards with difficult water removal characteristics, e.g., linerboard, fluting medium, foodboard, etc.

Figure 3.57. DOUBLE-FELTED UNI-DOUBLE-PRESS
This arrangement provides a sheet 5–8% drier than single felted presses used on webs with difficult water removal characteristics. Eliminates picking.

supplemented in certain cases by the addition of a press with high nip pressure. This applies especially to such grades as greaseproof, foodboard and similar grades which are difficult to press.

3.6 typical paperboard mills

The wide number of variations make it difficult to select for description what might be described as "typical examples" of paperboard machines in Europe. Inevitably since the majority of modern board machine installations are of a "combination" variety, the examples selected here for description are at least indicative of acceptable modern-type paperboard machines and their operation, even if it cannot be said that they are exactly typical—in the sense that no two board machines are ever the same practically speaking.

We will take a brief look at paperboard mill and machine operations in these countries: Australia, Denmark, Italy, Spain and Scotland.

1 The mill of our choice in Australia operates a Fourdrinier–Inverform machine combination, an interesting and most versatile arrangement used here in the conventional way for making single ply papers ranging from lightweight bag and wrapping grades. By bringing into use two Inverform stations, multi-ply paperboards for carton, corrugated and solid fibreboard conversion can also be made satisfactorily on the same machine. The actual paper-cum-board-machine has a rated 27,000 m/ tons yearly. It includes conventional suction press units, dryer section, size press (in 24th position of a set of 32 driers) and a winder. The main raw material pulps are: pelleted eucalypt NSSC—lapped eucalypt kraft— imported long fibred (softwood)—secondary fibres (wastepaper). The virgin pulp components are converted to a fibrous suspension in a Hi-Lo pulper and processed in double disc refiners. The wastepaper component is slushed in a Turboflex pulper equipped with trash removal facilities and is screened through diaphragm and pressure screens and cylindrical and cyclone-type cleaners. It is finally passed through a vertical de-flaker (see section 1.16.**2**), and being vertical this also accomplishes screening. From here, stock is thickened before passing to a pitch dispersal plant, the key unit of which is an Asplund Defibrator.

2 The mill chosen in Denmark for description operates a conventional Fourdrinier machine, 3·1 m wide, with an extra long machine wire (30 m) due to low drainage rate of the straw pulp furnish used in the

manufacture of high quality fluting medium. Extra drainage is achieved by the use of rotabelts under the forming wire. Press part and dryer are of conventional type. The raw material pulp is semichemical straw pulp (produced by the HF method described in section 1.6.**9**), in a mixture with wastepaper and semichemical woodpulp—the latter to facilitate machine-wire drainage and improve wet sheet strength at couch transfer. The stock preparation section operates two centrifugal pulpers, one for slushing waste paper and the other for reducing wood-pulp laps. The various pulp fibre components are blended and treated on a joint continuous basis—(straw pulp is screw fed into the system). Equipment includes: conical refiners, classifiers, two stage hydro-cyclones (centri-cleaners).

3 A typical mill in Italy is operating a 3 m wide, combined cylinder mould and Fourdrinier board machine with MG cylinder for the manufacture of double faced (white/white and white/grey) boxboards. Operating speed is between 15–85 m/min and rated capacity is around 30,000 tons per year. The arrangement was designed for maximum flexibility in output, substance range and "quality". The wet end comprises five cylinder moulds—for the back-ply, a suction uniflow, three others are contraflow of conventional design and construction without stock re-circulation; the intermediate ply-forming mould is operated in uniflow with recirculation. The cylinder mould press section is equipped with a bottom suction roll press and two plain presses. The Fourdrinier wire adds the top liner. It is 28 m long and followed by a straight through press with suction, and two reverse presses. The dryer section has 25 Fourdrinier standard type driers, and a dryer equipped with a felt (to relieve the MG's function) and an MG cylinder of 450 cm diameter. The last runs without a felt but has a high efficiency extraction hood. There follow 10 after-driers. Two cooling cylinders are located before a 5-roll calender stack, followed by a pope reel-up and cooler. Raw material pulps include wheat, straw NSSC, groundwood and waste paper. Stock preparation is accomplished by advanced central push button control and includes the following equipment: two centrifugal pulpers; refining lines each comprising—a de-flaker, two conical type refiners and a basalt filled disc refiner. A battery of de-flakers handles waste paper stock and mill prepared semichemical and groundwood pulps.

4 The Scottish installation comprises a 5-unit Inverform machine 3·5 m wide designed to produce 7 tons per hour of white lined chipboard, ivory plasterboard and lined manilla, and boxboard grades. This opera-tion was one of the first board machines to apply the topliner at the last Inverform station; virtually all other Inverform installations apply the topliner at the beginning. One of the express benefits (covered in section 3.4.**1**.14) is that there is no need to have the usual reserve press in the press section. This operating unit therefore only has straight through presses. There are five presses: 1st and 2nd primary suction presses; 1st main press (suction); 2nd main press (suction); and 3rd main press (plain). The main presses have granite top rolls; the other presses are rubber covered. There are 75 drying cylinders in five sections. A meter-

ing bar coater and breaker stack are included in the 3rd drying section. In the last section is a horizontal size press. Two 8-roll calender stacks follow, each with a bottom roll nip pressure of 61 kg/cm (345 lb per linear inch). A canopy-type extraction hood encloses the drying section.

5 One of the latest board mills erected in Spain at the time of writing is using a 4·2 m wide combined cylinder Fourdrinier arrangement with an MG cylinder. The single Fourdrinier wire is 21·3 m long. There are five dry vat cylinder mould units (125 cm dia). Rated output of boxboard grades—white lined chipboard, duplex, triplex foodboard; and test liner for corrugated container manufacture, is about 100 tons/day. Maximum speed is 120 m/min (400 ft/min). Multi-ply board basis weight range is 200–500 g/m². The web formed at the vats can be compressed at the intermediate press section. The first of these presses is a suction press, the second a plain press with rubber covered rolls. The web is now combined with the top layer from the Fourdrinier wire of conventional design. The main press section comprises a suction press and two reverse plain presses with granite top rolls. The drier section comprises 32 board dryers and five felt dryers. The MG cylinder is 4·5 m diameter and has a high velocity hood with a felt. There is a horizontal size press, a 3-roll calender stack, a metering bar coater and airknife wet-on-wet arrangement, a hot air drying tunnel, a 6-roll calender stack and a brush polishing unit. Raw material pulps are cellulose, groundwood and clean white waste paper. Two continuous pulpers treat the waste paper in a line consisting of: pulper, cyclones, classifiners, vorject and cyclone cleaners, selectifiers, and finally two gravity-type thickeners. De-fibration takes place in 5 de-flakers. Final stock refining takes place in 6 Jordans.

3.7 paperboard machine specifications

Although individual requirements will and do vary from mill to mill and between different countries and markets, the accompanying Table 3.2

Table 3.2. PAPERBOARD MACHINE SPECIFICATIONS

Trim wire width, mm	inches	Max. speed m min	Max. speed ft min	Capacity mt/day	Grade(s)
5,800	228	600	2,000	400	Fluting
6,450	254	700	2,300	500	Fluting
6,300	248	600	2,000	850	Linerboard
4,000	158	240	800	110	Linerboard
6,555	258	700	2,300	900	Kraftliner
4,550	179	300	1,000	270	Testliner and whitelined chipboard
3,900	154	120	400	100	Whitelined chip and folding boxboard
3,250	128	200	650	150	Folding boxboard
4,200	165	350	1,200	270	Folding boxboard

records typical vat/Fourdrinier paperboard machine specification details for a number of board grade machines which are on order or have been supplied between 1960 and 1970. The eight countries involved are: America, Bulgaria, Canada, Finland, Hungary, Italy, Spain, USSR.

4 | mineral coating of paperboard

4.1 reasons for mineral coating

Owing to the nature of paperboard as related to the natural characteristics of its cellulosic components, all machine-made paperboards are to varying degrees "anisotropic" (non-uniform) in structure. The type of mechanical treatment to which the fibres have been subjected during preparation does not basically affect this.

Because of the two sided sheet characteristics inherent in normal machine-made paperboards, it is common to supplement the natural surface texture by coating with certain minerals to provide an ideal smooth and ink receptive surface for the true rendering of print, colour and halftone work and in the treatment of certain packaging applications. It is worthwhile to list some of the specific reasons for coating paperboards:

To improve surface receptivity to print.

To mask original surface characteristics of some grades of paperboard.

To reduce abrasion and the tendency towards fluffing and picking of the fibres during printing.

To upgrade the texture of a sheet made from a lower grade fibrous furnish, e.g., waste paper.

To produce an attractive box or carton with a good sales appeal.

The above list covers principally those reasons for "surface" coating—sometimes also referred to as "printable clay-type coating". This type of coating application is distinct from "functional" coating.

Functional coatings are generally interpreted as coatings which impart barrier-type protective properties and/or physical (material)-type properties. They are generally applied to the side opposite the printable pigmented coatings, but they may be applied to both sides of paper, film, foil, or board.

Barrier-type properties are: grease resistance, water resistance, water vapour resistance and resistance to gas permeation. The physical or material-type functional properties are many and include:

Slip.
Anti-slip.
Non-abrasion.
Abrasion or scuff resistance.
Release.
Block resistance.
Heat sealability.
High gloss, clarity, etc.

The functional coating of boxes and cartons is covered in Chapter 5.

4.2 surface properties: mechanical characteristics

The anisotropy of paper and paperboard is important in its influence on the development of an ideal printing surface, in terms both of the uncoated paperboard web or sheet and body board for subsequent coating. Any irregularities in surface texture, grammage, thickness, bulk and optical properties will have a direct bearing on the degree of receptivity of the coating slip. The freeness/wetness values and the amount of capillary attraction of the fibres all play a large part in the redistribution of the coating vehicle into the body paper.

Any coating which is applied to an uneven surface will usually result in severe difficulties during printing. It is usual to apply certain weights of coating according to the degree of penetration of the printing ink to be used, so that the ink vehicle penetrates to the depth of the coating. If the coating is deposited on a rough, uneven, fibrous layer, then the ink vehicle cannot penetrate uniformly with the result that the print will lose definition.

When it is required to produce the best possible printing surface by mineral coating, then a double application is advisable. There are various methods by which this can be achieved and almost any of the modern coating processes can be used. A typical example includes the application of the first coat by means of a blade coater, followed by airknife to gauge the depth of the coating and give even coverage. It is of interest to note that the airknife process may be characterized because the coating conforms to the surface of the substrate. Hence it is possible with this machine to coat a paper or board while still retaining the original pattern. This also illustrates the necessity of having a smooth surface in the first place, if it is desired to produce the best even result.

MAIN REQUIREMENTS OF PAPERBOARD FOR COATING

1 Uniformity of formation.
2 Uniformity of finish, grammage and thickness.

3 Good dimensional stability with a moisture content of about 7–8%, to ensure a level, curl and cockle free sheet.

4.3 selecting a mineral coating material

Basically a *coating colour* can be divided into two phases. The liquid phase is the adhesive or binder and the suspended phase the coating mineral. The importance of these phases will be seen later and the primary considerations in the selection of a coating revolve around the following:

1 For high white, tinted and bright coatings, the pigment particles should scatter light with the minimum of light absorption. This property is controlled by the ratio between the refractive indices of the pigment and the binder, also the number of pigment particles per unit area. This is itself dependent on the thickness of the coating.

2 The requirement for opacity in any one coating formulation is primarily governed by the variations in the refractive indices of its essential components, which include the pigment, binder and air. Thus the higher the refractive index of the pigment over that of the binder and air, the greater the opacity or hiding power of the coating. Conversely, the greater the replacement of the air by a binder which has a refractive index approaching that of the pigment, the lower the opacity of the coating. It is, therefore, necessary to maintain a high ratio between the pigment and the binder if optimum opacity is desired.

3 Brightness is similarly affected by the ratio of pigment to binder.

4 The requirement for smoothness, which is an essential in printing grades, is determined by paper hardness and surface contour. In order to achieve smoothness by calendering, it is important that the adhesive to pigment ratio of the coating slip is correct for a particular set of conditions. Any variation in this ratio and also in the type of pigment used will produce a variation in the finish. Excessive adhesive will reduce the finish, as the coating will pass from the plastic to the solid phase.

Not all pigments are equally well suited for use in a coating mix owing to their different physical structure, i.e., particle size, shape and hardness. The harder a pigment, the more difficult becomes the action of calendering, owing to the necessity for greater compression values. These in turn set up varying degrees of permanent set (irreversible compression). This phenomenon accounts for the high percentage of china clay used in coating formulations which, because of its physical structure (mica-like platelets), allows a very high degree of smoothness to be obtained without the need for excessive pressure and deformation.

BINDERS IN COMMON USE. The object of the binder or adhesive is to "fix" the pigment to the paperboard and to itself. It also controls the viscosity of the coating slip and thus the flexibility of the final coating. The flow properties of a coating mix depend on the nature of the pigment, dispersing agents used and the type and quantity of the adhesive and the ultimate pigment adhesive equilibrium. The adhesive also has an influence on the absorption of water and the degree of receptivity of the printing ink.

The most generally used binders are in the form of starch and casein. Starch tends to form weak bonds with a resultant brittle coating allied to low flexibility. The use of synthetic latices as major constituents of the binder element of the coating has led to better bending properties of coated paperboard. Improved ink hold out also results.

4.4 the effects of the rheological properties of coatings

There are three properties of viscosity associated with coating formulations, which are known as Newtonian, thixotropic and dilatant.

Newtonian fluids maintain a constant viscosity while subjected to varying rates of hydraulic shear. However, in the case of thixotropic solutions, these exhibit the property of decreasing viscosity, which is accelerated by the rate of shear. The opposite effect takes place with dilatant suspensions whereby the viscosity increases with increase in the rate of shear, which can develop to a solid gel state, particularly when the solids concentration is high, which is often the case.

Such viscous properties are of particular importance when related to the application of coatings, in view of the high speeds at which many coating machines and processes operate. Most coating methods, in particular those incorporating roll application, produce elevated conditions of hydraulic shear at the point of application of the coating to the web. It is, therefore, obvious that whatever the viscous nature of a particular coating may be, this must be sufficiently fluid to enable its application at high speeds to give smooth and complete coverage of the web. Thus the effects of thixotropy and dilatancy of the coating may be observed in the surface of the paperboard. A tendency a coating has towards dilatacy will become apparent by the development of pattern marks (orange peel) on the surface. With thixotropic coatings difficulty can be experienced owing to the problem of the binder vehicle not having time to completely enter the "body" with the result that the coating weight deposited is less than required.

4.5 functional coating and/or laminating

Functional coating and/or laminating has the capability of imparting important properties to paperboard materials. Such properties can be listed as follows:

> Grease resistance.
> Moisture vapour resistance.
> Gas and odour resistance.
> Heat resistance.
> Water resistance.
> Chemical resistance.
> Wet strength.
> Dry-sheet strength—stiffness and rigidity.
> Print receptive surface.
> Visual appeal.

The above listing is not exhaustive nor suggestive of priorities. Specific properties such as inherent wet strength, heat resistance and certain dry sheet properties are imparted by the use of strong pulps and suitable pulp blends. The last two properties listed are achieved or enhanced by "on machine" pigment coating and other surface treatments.

The choice between coating or laminating naturally depends on numerous factors. The main point to remember is that properties like "printability", surface appearance, body absorption (for glueing), scuffing resistance, etc., are not affected by lamination.

We will consider the important aspects of some individual functional requirements of paperboard as introduced earlier. Table 4.1 shows the relative advantages of several functional coatings in common use.

Table 4.1. SUGGESTED COATINGS

PROPERTY	SHORT SHELF LIFE		LONG TERM STORAGE	
	uncreased	creased	uncreased	creased
Barrier to oxygen Nitrogen and Carbon Dioxide	PVDC, EVA/wax compounds, Polyethylene	PVDC, EVA/wax compounds, Polyethylene	PVDC, EVA/wax compounds, Polyethylene	PVDC, EVA/wax compounds, Polyethylene
Barrier to moisture vapour	PVDC, Polyethylene, EVA/wax compounds, paraffin wax	Polyethylene, EVA/micro/ paraffin/wax, PVDC	PVDC, Polyethylene, EVA/wax compounds, paraffin wax	Polyethylene, EVA/micro/ paraffin wax, PVDC
Resistance to acids	Polypropylene polyethylene, PVC, wax/EVA compound	—	Polypropylene polyethylene, PVC, wax/EVA compound	—
Resistance to alkali	Polypropylene, Micro/paraffin/wax, Polyethylene, Polyethylene compound, PVC	—	Polypropylene, Polyethylene, Polyethylene compound, PVC	—
Resistance to mineral oil	Unplasticized PVC, Polypropylene PVA, EVA/wax compounds, PVDC	Unplasticized PVC, PVC	Unplasticized PVC, Polypropylene, PVA PVA, EVA/wax compounds	Unplasticized PVC, Polypropylene
Resistance to vegetable oils and animal fats	Polyethylene, Polypropylene	Polyethylene, Polypropylene	Polypropylene	Polypropylene

4.6 functional requirements of paperboards

4.6.1 Grease resistance

Grease resistance is an important functional requirement of many paperboards, particularly in connection with the prevention of staining of cartons. Staining is likely to occur in cartoning inherently greasy products like bakery produce, butter, fats, etc. Engineering parts, greased and oiled, also fall within this range. However, some distinction must be made between grease *resistance* and grease *proofness*. The latter calls for a coating fully inert to direct contact with greases. Thus, materials containing waxes and poly-ethylene are precluded, but are often suitable in boards with a lower degree of grease resistance. For true "greaseproofness", materials commonly used include: unplasticized PVC, PVDC, polypropylene, or similar plastic coatings. In addition, certain hot melts based on ethylene/vinyl acetate copolymers in conjunction with extenders will also provide a necessary degree of grease resistance. Hygiene is an important consideration.

An important practical aspect of the grease resistant properties of a carton concern its creasing. It is desirable that grease does not penetrate through creases, especially if it be present in a fluid state. In such situations it is necessary to have an absorbent inner board surface. The grease resistant barrier may have to be built into the board centre or be transferred to the outside of the carton.

An ideally effective barrier, with visual merit, involves white or opaque polyethylene for the carton outside. Extruded polypropylene although more costly exhibits improved grease resistance to mineral oils and greases over polyethylene. It is, nevertheless, well suited to longer term shelf life especially with pharmaceuticals—ointments, etc.

4.6.2 *Moisture vapour resistance*

Moisture affects a great many packaged products. It is frequently manifest through product drying, softening, swelling, corrosion, etc. Thus, inner package conditions relative to product compatibility vary widely. Polyvinylidene chloride is an excellent coating material for moisture vapour resistance—MVR. It can be applied in aqueous dispersion as a heavy coating (30–50 g/m^2) on normal density board, or 15–25 g/m^2 on denser stock. Also, it is applicable to a glassine/wax/board laminate construction at near 10–20 g/m^2. This makes a costly package, however. Dispersion with PVDC is expensive, but is nevertheless often justified in the packaging of soluble beverages, powdered cream, etc.

Wax blends and polyethylene also provide a high MVR. However, the usage of wax blends tends to be giving way to wax-copolymer hot melt compounds or polyethylene, as these more easily produce a pinhole free film than the simple wax blends.

Polyethylene has good visual properties. It can be applied as a clear coating, often over a bleached faced board already printed, or as pigmented coating applied directly on the board machine, e.g., unlined chipboard. It is not much affected by carton creasing.

High MVR, particularly in the creased state, is also achieved through the use of ethylene/vinyl copolymers in blends with paraffin and microcrystalline waxes. These have the advantage that application can be by normal hot melt coating equipment. Recent carton constructions, coated on the inside with polyethylene or similar high barrier materials, are for instance being used to contain soft drinks, etc.

4.6.3 *Gas and odour resistance*

Food product odour tainting is a serious problem with certain common food products like fish, meat, cheese. Barrier properties can be provided through coating or lamination. Coatings are frequently blended with paraffin or microcrystalline waxes and other resins. Laminations offer high barrier properties using wax miscible copolymers of EVA, and using polyethylene.

F(

4.6.**4** *Heat resistance*

Polypropylene in particular has a high melting point well above that of other plastic coatings. Foil lining by lamination to board also provides an excellent heat barrier.

This laminate is commonly used in bake-in-carton packs for cake mixes, etc.

4.6.**5** *Water resistance*

This property can be achieved by wax coating, by the use of hot melts or by laminating using foil, polyethylene or bitumen. The last is not acceptable for food packaging, however, its advantage being largely one of cheapness.

Wax lamination has much to favour it. Economy is the principal merit. Relatively high wax viscosity is necessary for suitable lamination and this can be achieved by the addition to the wax blend of adhesive-giving polymers, e.g., butyl rubber, copolymers, etc. Their presence prevents absorption of the adhesive into the bodyboard and imparts flexibility and cohesive strength with good barrier properties when creased.

Polyethylene is used for much the same purpose as wax laminant compounds. It has the chief advantage that MVR can be varied easily according to the gauge of the polyethylene used. It is not dependent as a process on the characteristics of the substrate and is frequently used to impart a higher finish to already off-machine coated carton board.

Extruding polyethylene on carton stock is also practised where the cost is justified. An instance is soft drink cartons—see Volume 2.

4.6.**6** *Chemical resistance*

Wax based compounds and polyolefines are basically inert to most chemicals. Polyethylene is commonly used as already described along with wax compounds.

4.6.**7** *Wet strength*

Wet strength agents as may normally be added to paperboard furnish naturally improve the basic board material. It may be further improved by laminating to a wet-strength paper. Adhesives used must be highly resistant to water such as synthetic resin glues, e.g., styrene-butadiene/casein mixture, etc.

4.6.**8** *Dry sheet strength*

This has been adequately covered in earlier chapters. However, board "strength" can be measurably improved through lamination of a variety of different characteristic boards.   MD/CD strength ratios are easily altered by laminating. Board grain ratios can be reduced by 50% through lamination in some cases.

4.7 **functional coating materials**

We will here briefly consider some of the major functional coating materials.

4.7.1 *Polyvinylidene chloride* (PVDC)

Usually this is available as copolymers of vinylidene chloride with vinyl chloride or acrylates, and it gives an excellent barrier to moisture vapour, gas, grease, etc. It is replacing certain laminates, e.g., glassine/wax/board combinations and to some extent wax and polyethylene compounds. It is especially suited for printing on. Often, it can serve as an overprint varnish and barrier coat combined. This latter capability is of special advantage in the manufacture of cartons for dry foods, for example, where the prime need is to prevent entry of moisture into the carton, rather than egress of grease from the contents.

Coating applications involve much skill. The usual process is airknife. Careful after-drying is important. Fusion temperature is important. Working on the precoat theory, better results are obtained if a barrier coat, often of PVC, is given to paperboard first. However, the coater needs three stations, because PVDC needs at least two coats. Thickeners can be used to improve PVDC coverage on board. This enhances appearance as well as improving barrier properties for a given coat weight.

4.7.2 *Polyethylene*

Medium density polyethylene is normally used in the coating of paperboards. It is widely used on frozen food cartons. Pigmented polyethylene as an outer coating imparts high gloss to the surface lending it readily to printing. Such coatings can be in various colours and also are well suited to embossing. Special effects can be obtained by incorporation of metal flake powder (aluminium or bronze) in the poly coating, which also maintains its barrier properties.

4.7.3 *Paraffin wax*

Paraffin wax is one of the oldest used protective coatings against moisture. It has several advantages; it is cheap, easy to apply, two side coating simultaneously is possible and at high speed. Disadvantages include brittleness (flaking of coated board) and difficulty in glueing.

The addition of microcrystalline wax, polyethylene, EVA copolymers, etc., to paraffin wax have largely overcome the shortcomings mentioned. However, the increase in viscosity of the coating blend consequent upon addition of these "additives" limits somewhat their addition.

4.7.4 *Microcrystalline wax*

Microcrystalline wax is a good laminating material that imparts high barrier properties. The addition of rubber-type polymers increases its adhesive properties and also prevents wicking of the wax into porous board and into its liner, so causing discoloration. These materials are relatively inexpensive and are ideally suited to machinery designed to laminate chipboard to a variety of lining papers at high speed.

4.7.5 *Hot melts*

Hot melts cover a blend of thermoplastic resins and copolymers *extended* by crystalline and paracrystalline waxes. They are widely used to coat fibreboard container and folding carton blanks and are separately dealt with in Volume 2.

4.8 coating practice and machine developments

4.8.1 *On-machine coating developments*

Within the last few years, on-paperboard machine coating developments have advanced significantly. Speeds of operation have improved greatly, yet "quality" has been maintained and often improved. The new generation coaters are designed for and run at higher speeds. It is not unusual to reach speeds of 1,000 m/min. This is being achieved largely owing to the more thorough understanding of coating technology and the practice that has now been acquired. In addition, there has taken place a distinct practical improvement in the mechanical aspects of production and coater designs.

The real benefits of coating are today recognized to lie in the technique of applying the "absolute" lightest coating weight that will still be sufficient to satisfactorily upgrade "performance quality" of paperboards in a functional sense. The lighter the weight of coating applied the lower the cost.

There is in consequence today a very noticeable trend towards multi-station coating. A typical coating arrangement is seen in Fig. 4.1. Many mills are noticed to favour blade/airknife coating arrangements and combination coating.

4.8.2 *Multi-station coating*

The concept of multi-station coating follows the pre-coat theory. This maintains that a "better" board is produced if the surface is firstly pre-coated and is then followed by another coating than is generally found to be the case if the whole coating weight is applied in one step. Multiple coating is a desirable and acceptable means of lowering costs.

4.8.2.1 BLADE/AIRKNIFE COATING

A typical multi-station coating arrangement, for instance, operating on a German board machine, includes two coating heads for each side of the sheet—a total of four coating applications. This permits a 7–10 g/m² coating per side at an inverted blade station, followed by a 15–30 g/m² application at an airknife station. Base paper substance ranges from 80–300 g/m².

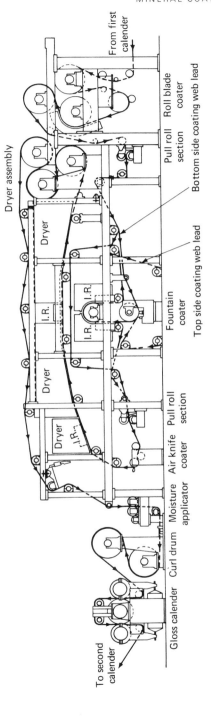

Figure 4.1. MULTI-STATION COATING ARRANGEMENT

The popularity of multi-station coating lines follows the pre-coat theory. Seen here is a three station pigment coating arrangement.

Paperboard mills require great built-in production flexibility today in order to produce a wide range of coated board grades demanded by their markets. An advantage of multi-station coaters, e.g., blade/airknife, is that the coating weight range can vary from, say, 8 to 40 g/m^2 per side. This is simply achieved in the bypassing of certain coating heads. Thus, it is acceptable to have three coating heads on a machine, e.g., metering bar, blade and airknife, for one side coating board.

4.8.2.2 BLADE-ON-BLADE COATING

Blade-on-blade coating is also becoming more popular. This arrangement produces a highly uniform and well bound coating at speeds up to 500 m/min. Also blade-on-blade permits a lower cost coating application than is the case with one heavy coat from a single blade station.

4.8.2.3 FOUR STAGE MULTI-COATING

Indicative of the growing trend towards multi-station coating is the following example, of what, at the time of writing, is believed to be the only board machine to report four-stage on-machine coating. The arrangement is: bar coater, roll coater, bar coater and airknife, in combination with infra-red drying and a glazing cylinder. The machine is able to make all grades of MG and coated board, and of duplex board. The product is primarily used for postcards and luxury packages. Trimmed board machine width is 290 cm, and production is between 90–125 tons/day. This is much higher than is usually found with this grade of board.

4.8.2.4 SIZE PRESS AND PRE-COATING DEVICES

The size press as a pre-coating arrangement along with other pre-coating devices is receiving renewed interest. This is particularly the case with design units that coat both sides of the sheet at once.

4.9 off-machine coating developments

Apart from certain traditional off-machine coating methods that today are somewhat of a speciality nature like cast coating, brush coating, and a few others of rather less significance, the majority of pigment coating methods/processes used are basically identical in their important features. Off-machine pigment coating applications certainly are today becoming more confined to a narrower range of speciality paperboards than was the case some years ago. This is largely because improvements in the technical knowledge has allowed a considerable upgrading of paperboard materials to take place directly on the paperboard machine, at far greater economies than was ever possible before. Therefore, the desirability or need to use off-machine coating process has in many cases been greatly reduced. Also a great many more "economy-of-scale" production paperboards are today being coated as a matter of course. This is mainly through a number of light weight coat applications at high speed on the board machine, used to impart specific functional and often aesthetic characteristics to the board surface. Formerly these individual properties were either not required or, if they were, it was often not for the same purposes as imposed by the markets of today.

Also, a trend is taking place towards a more widespread use of "combined" coating arrangements. These may be either on- or off-machine. A distinction must here be made, however, between multi-coating arrangements and "combined" coating arrangements. In the former sense, we are talking about several basically similar coating methods, in combination. For example, a three or four station pigment coating arrangement on a board machine might typically consist of: size press-metering bar-blade-airknife coating stations. According to the requirements of the coated sheet, one or more of these stations can simply be bypassed during the coating operation. Obviously such an arrangement, which is quite common, has a relatively high degree of production/quality flexibility—another reason underlying the trend towards multi-coating.

In contrast, a "combined" coating arrangement would be distinguishable, in that it is most likely an off-machine operation, though not necessarily so. Typical of a so-called "combination" set up is the pigment coater/extruder featured in Figs. 4.20(a)(b) Volume 2. Maximum "printability" is obtained with this paperboard coating arrangements using a single trailing blade coater. The same arrangement includes provision for polyethylene extrusion, where desirable barrier properties for packaging applications are provided.

This latter type of coating/extruding arrangement (although it can conceivably be linked up to a paperboard machine, somewhere near the reel wind up end occasionally on an elevated floor, see Fig. 3.41), is not particularly well suited to on-machine production because of the speed of operation. Also a major disadvantage in the case of non-pigmented coatings lies in the re-use of coated broke in the stock preparation system. This presents an uneconomic and practical problem. It is also the principal reason, as such, for the unit being an off-machine operation.

In addition to the coater/extruder type of arrangement described, there is also in operation at the present time a multi-coater/laminator arrangement as described in section 5.4. There is no apparent reason why such or similar arrangements will not increase both in numbers and in the sophistication of their functional purpose in the future. In fact, the number of such individually tailored arrangements is expected to become legion in a very short time. However, the basic principles are not themselves expected to show much change.

4.10 on-line coating arrangements

A few years back, coating arrangements were classified basically as "on-" or "off-machine" installations. However, developments that have since taken place in both coating know-how and technology, allied to the consumer and packaging demands of a more sophisticated society, are tending to blur the former distinction. Board makers have found it possible to build on-line coating arrangements following the board machine, such that the coating function can be performed either directly on the board machine web, or as a separate treatment after winding. The suitability of this flexible type of coating combination depends very much on the uses to which the board is to be put. This is what will largely determine the type, quality and requirements of a particular coating application.

4.11 coating methods: "on-machine"

On-machine coating methods in current use in paperboard mills are indicated in Table 4.2.

4.11.1 *Size press pigment coating*

The size press, Figs. 4.2 and 4.3, has nowadays become more or less standard equipment on paper and paperboard machines of the Fourdrinier—Fourdrinier-combination and MG type. Size presses are rarely used in cylinder board manufacture.

Originally, size presses were intended only for a sizing application, to improve the surface of a sheet with regard to: water resistance of writing and printing qualities; improved resistance to grease; oil; etc. However, the traditional size press is now commonly used for the application of pigment coating to papers and paperboard.

A particular disadvantage in using a size press for pigment coating lies in the low limit to coating weight application, and also the low solids content relative to other coating processes. The usual maximum coating weight does not exceed 10 g/m² per side. However, for certain coating applications the size press is adequate. It is frequently used to give a so-called "wash" of coating to the surface of paperboards. This is by way of a slight upgrading in surface properties, such as may be required on certain grades of white lined chipboard, etc.

In the sense of this usual type of wash coating application, one or more size presses are commonly used for applying a "surface treatment", ahead of some other types of coater. A size press may, nevertheless, be considered a coater by itself.

4.11.2 *Size press design*

Size presses come in two types—a vertical and a horizontal arrangement of press rolls. These are simply a pair of squeeze rolls, which force size or coating into the surface of the sheet and simultaneously express a flooded surplus. Depending on the roll arrangement, ahead of the press nip, a coating barrier is formed through which the web passes.

As in the mechanics of all coating processes, there are a number of size press designs and performance variables. In principle, these variables are the same whether or not the press be used as a size applicator and/or coater. They are adequately discussed in literature available elsewhere and are omitted mention here.

Table 4.2 COMMON ON-MACHINE PAPERBOARD COATERS

Coater details	Size press 1	Airknife 2	Champion metering bar 3
A Sketch			
B Average single coating per side weight, g/m²	3–10	P 5–35 B 5–30	2·5–14
C Solids content, %	10–35	P 40–52 B 35–45	25–55
D Speed, ft/min, m/min	1000 300	1200 400	B 500 167
E Viscosity range, cP	up to 300	50–500	50–1000 and higher
F Deckles	No	Yes	Yes
G After-drying convection (C) or drums (D)	C+D	C	C+D
H Results and comments	Good for prime coat—or medium price coated grades—has surface pattern	Top coat contour coater—wide range coating weights—tunnel dryer required depends on coating weights	Prime coat—board grades—wide range products

	Champflex 5	Pond blade 6	Flexiblade 7	Flooded nip and Inverta blade 8	Controlled fountain 9
A					
B	5–7	8–10	8–10	11–14	11–14
C	50–55	50–62	50–65	50–65	50–65
D	1000 300	4000	3500 1200	3500 1200	5000 1700
E	50–11,000	1000–40,000	1000–40,000	1000–15,000	15–50,000
F	No	Yes	Yes	Yes	No
G	C	C	C	C	C
H	Art coated—food and packaging boards	Light coated	Prime coat—paper, boards, food and packaging boards	Art coated—food and packaging boards	Art grades, board—functional coatings wide range

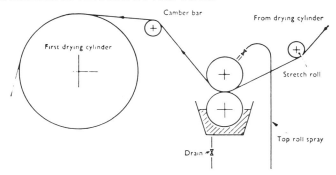

Figure 4.2.   VERTICAL SIZE PRESS LICK-UP ROLL APPLICATION TO UNDERSIDE

Figure 4.3.   HORIZONTAL SIZE PRESS
One of a pair of presses running on a board machine to size the top and back liners separately.

4.11.3 *Airknife coaters*

Originally the airknife, Figs. 4.4(a)(b)(c)(d), 4.5 and 4.6, was developed as an off-machine coater, for the production of slightly "lower" quality coated grades than conventional brush coated art. With slight modification the method is used extensively as an on-machine installation.

Undoubtedly the airknife coater is the most versatile of all coating units handling water based coatings. Airknife will handle mineral coatings, functional barrier coatings, silicone release coatings, etc. The simplest design airknife coater is used for board coating.

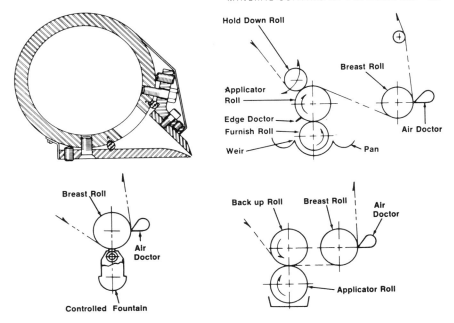

Figure 4.4(a).   AIRKNIFE COATER CROSS SECTION
Figure 4.4(b).   AIRKNIFE COATER WITH TWO ROLL KISS APPLICATOR WITH FURNISH ROLL
Figure 4.4(c).   AIRKNIFE COATER WITH FOUNTAIN APPLICATOR
Figure 4.4(d).   AIRKNIFE COATER WITH SQUEEZE APPLICATOR

The design consists of a pick up roll which applies an excess quantity of coating to the web. This excess coating is afterwards removed by a narrow stream of air issuing from the airknife blade onto the board surface backed up by a web supporting roll.

Airknife is a contour coater. Its particular characteristic is that during coating the knife tends to apply the same weight of coating on the "hills" as it does in the "valleys" of the sheet. With the advent of wet-on-wet coating techniques of boards to produce better results with packaging grades, the airknife is used in conjunction with a blade or metering bar coater. The latter applies a "filler" coat, the contour of which is followed by the airknife. A wide range of coating weights may be applied. For coating board grades, a maximum weight of 30 g/m² at 45% solids content is average.

Ultimate success in airknife operation is due fully to the rheological properties of the coating. Although capable of operating at speeds up to 2,000 ft/min, this coater is frequently restricted to 1,300 ft/min owing to severe misting with clay coatings. The real limitation of the airknife is its inability to handle coatings with high solids content, not so much because of the high solids, but because of the high viscosity generally associated with them.

Therefore, a high percentage of water must be evaporated. This calls for careful and low drying rates, a negligible factor in off-machine coating but a serious limitation on board machines.

Figure 4.5.   AIRKNIFE COATER
Airknife coating most commonly follows a blade coater. Seen here, coating solid bleached board, it is the second coating stage installed on-line with an Inverform machine and follows the blade coating station shown in Fig. 4.13. The airknife (air jet) extends across the whole web width of 375 cm trimmed deckle.

What makes an airknife a desirable coater is largely its ability to apply an absolutely uniform layer of coating, free of mottle and other surface blemishes and over a fairly wide range of coating weights. Use of airknife coaters is made in applying a surface colour tint to change surface appearance. At the same time it has the ability to apply an improved form of printing surface with, if necessary, additional properties such as grease resistance, sensitizing, etc.

4.11.4 *Metering bar coaters*

Metering bar or rod coaters, Figs. 4.7 and 4.8, are today all patterned on the first patented design Champion coater. Different models using a similar principle are currently available on the market.

The metering bar coater is a popular model. The machine shown in Fig. 4.7 is designed so that the web follows a lead in roll and passes over an applicator roll rotating in a trough, and onward to the metering bar. Here excess coating is wiped off, leaving a smooth coated surface to be dried. The unit is designed to have adjustable wrap-angles on the applicator roll and metering bar.

Figure 4.6.   AIRKNIFE COATER

The installation shown here is part of a wet-on-wet coating arrangement following a metering bar unit on a board machine.

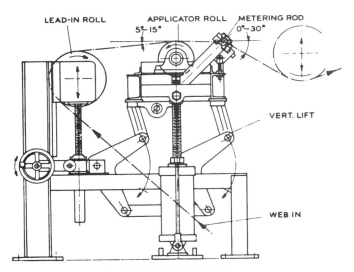

Figure 4.7.   METERING ROD OR BAR COATER (PRINCIPLE)

Figure 4.8.   METERING BAR COATER
The arrangement seen here can be operated either on- or off-machine. It works here in conjunction with a wet-on-wet airknife station.

Formerly, most board machines employed two coaters of this type, each with intermediate drying. This was so that single side and double coated grades could be produced.

Usually a single coating application is not sufficient for a prime printing grade surface. It is usual to consider the first coat basically as a priming coat, used to fill in wire marks, inter-fibre voids, etc. The metering bar generally wipes most coating off any high spots, thereby improving board smoothness. A second coating application aims to provide a more uniform surface by better coverage. Latterly, airknife coating application has found favour for applying the second coat. This is frequently done in a "wet-on-wet" position, i.e., the coating that is applied at a previous station is not fully dried out— Fig. 4.6.

Because bar coaters are generally only able to control low coating weights (in the region of 2·5–14 g/m² per side), their most important characteristics lie in their tendency towards improving board surface smoothness, while applying a coating, plus extreme inbuilt simplicity of operation and compactness. Also they are relatively inexpensive machines.

4.11.5 *Blade coaters*

Considerable developments have occurred in blade coaters. There are, however, a number of machinery design variations. All, however, utilize a large diameter rubber covered back up roll to support a web while coating and metering. All blade coaters apply a viscose, high solids content (50–65%) coating in excess. This excess is then sliced off with a blade, which simultaneously presses coating into inter-fibre voids and surface irregularities and blemishes of the web, leaving behind a thin surface coating.

One of the early blade coaters was the pond-type (puddle) trailing blade process, Fig. 4.9. This was followed by the flexiblade, flooded nip and the fountain blade coaters. The main differences in all the blade coaters in current use is found to lie in the manner of applying coating to the web ahead of the flexible blade.

The blade coaters most favoured today utilize controlled application of coating in one step, followed by controlled metering with a knife blade. This can either be by way of using a rotating roll in a trough, for actual web control (controlled by coating roll speed), in conjunction with a blade to remove excess, or by way of a pressurized fountain to apply coating through an orifice, again using an independently isolated and adjustable blade to remove excess. Other methods include: coating feed through a nozzle, and a reverse driven smoothing roll. This has the advantage of exceptional control without film splitting or patterning which might cause differential absorption of coating before metering.

Unquestionably, the original blade coating development has today become a very sophisticated operation. Coating derives much of its popularity from a happy combination of certain desirable characteristics. These principally include: mechanically practical, high speed operational ability to use high solids formulation; application of a very smooth coating surface with web surface irregularities filled; low drying loads and high drying weights.

The three types of blade coaters now to be described are those generally found in use today in the mineral coating of paperboards.

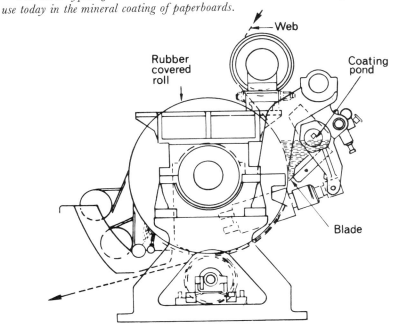

Figure 4.9. TRAILING BLADE (PUDDLE) COATER (PRINCIPLE)

Figure 4.10.   FLOODED NIP COATER

Seen here in detail is a flooded nip off-machine installation of designed speed 610 m/min. The rubber-covered applicator roll (370 mm) applies coating to the web passing round a 960 mm rubber-covered backing roll. Like the applicator roll, the inverted blade assembly is air loaded.

Figure 4.11.   HIGH SPEED FLOODED NIP COATER

Overall view from unwind end of off-machine flooded nip coater seen in detail in Fig. 4.10. The air cap is seen in detail in Fig. 4.14. The machine coats paper and bleached boards for food cartons, etc.

4.11.5.1 FLEXIBLADE

The Flexiblade was a direct development of the pond coater, in that the coating is contained in a pond (totally enclosed). Blade angle is 45°.

4.11.5.2 FLOODED NIP

Here, as seen in Fig. 4.10, the essential feature is a rubber covered backing roll, applicator roll and inverted blade. In operation the applicator roll runs in a pan at 10–25% of web speed, applies an excess to the sheet, which is then wiped off by the inverted trailing blade.

The term flooded nip comes from the hydraulic pressure developed between the applicator roll and the web on the backing roll. The gap is usually 0·1–0·4 mm (0·004–0·016 in). The pressure developed breaks aeration bubbles and eliminates "skip" caused by foaming. Blade angle is usually 35–65°.

A wide range of coating weights can be applied, e.g., 5–14 g/m² per side. The process is particularly suited to large and small orders.

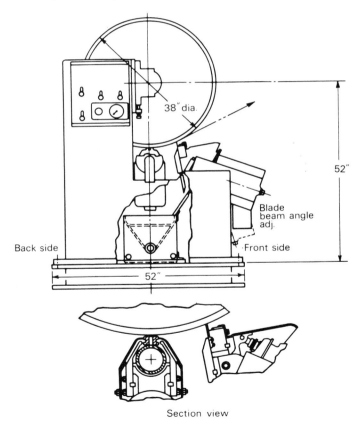

Section view

Figure 4.12. CONTROLLED FOUNTAIN BLADE COATER (PRINCIPLE)

Figure 4.13.   CONTROLLED FOUNTAIN BLADE COATER
Blade coating followed by airknife (Fig. 4.5) is a proven and very successful combination. In the blade coater shown here, the coating is applied by a so-called fountain and then levelled out under a flexible blade to a smooth base and is high velocity air-dried before the next coating application. The unit illustrated is actually part of an on-line paperboard machine (Inverform) arrangement producing solid bleached board of high grade for frozen food cartons, etc.

4.11.5.3   CONTROLLED FOUNTAIN BLADE COATER

This is the latest inverted blade coater to be developed. The orifice fountain with smoothing lip is completely separate from the blade. Application of the colour is by means of a variable delivery pump which applies a controlled excess. A second degree of control is derived from the precisely *balanced* loading of the unsupported fountain against the web. This floats on the coating film laid on the surface of the sheet. A wide range of coatings from very low (25 cps) to very high (50,000 cps) viscosity can be handled.

4.11.5.4   CHAMPFLEX COATER

In the Champflex coater, the web passes upwards over two oppositely revolving chrome plated pick up rolls, which apply an excess of coating to the sheet. The coating retained on the sheet surface is then metered by a small plated oppositely rotating roll head (10–20 rev/min), held in light contact with the web by the action of a spring clip. Coating weight is controlled by the speed of the applicator rolls, the diameter of the metering rod and pressure of the rod against the resilient backing roll. A second metering roll located on the opposite side of the backing roll can be used to apply a small amount of starch or coating to the opposite side of the web. Coating colour is pumped to the top pan at 50–55% solids, and overflows into the second applicator pan and on to recirculation. About 23 g/m² coating weight can be applied to paper up to 136–340 m/min (400–1,000 ft/min) and board at 60–170 m/min (175–500 ft/min). As with most coating methods, two lightweight coatings provide final results superior to one heavy coating application.

4.12 off-machine coating methods

An equal degree of sophistication has also taken place in off-machine coating techniques as with on-machine processes.

A number of coating systems in fact are processes common to both on- and off-machine installations. These are airknife, roll systems and blade coating methods.

4.13 drying

Slow, natural drying is the ideal and most technologically efficient method as it is considered that, by exposure to high temperatures, coated webs lose some of their quality.

Traditional coating methods rely on the use of festoon drying, which is virtually universally employed with brush coated papers. The maximum speed at which festoon drying may be satisfactorily carried out is about 100 m/min (300 ft/min). This limits the rate of production and calls for considerable floor space.

Figure 4.14.   HIGH VELOCITY AIR CAP

The most common and economical means of drying today is by the use of tunnels. These are insulated enclosures through which the web passes and where it is dried by streams of warm air. The most satisfactory type dries the coating in a single pass, but sometimes to save space or expense the web is returned through the same tunnel.

Each section of the tunnel is complete with heaters (usually steam coils) and fans to both feed in air and remove it. The air is blown through the heaters into a pressure chamber. It is then forced out through nozzles or slits at even pressure across the width of the machine. The design of the orifices and the angle at which they are set are most important factors in satisfactory dryer operation. Air is normally recirculated throughout the dryer and in practice very little has to be exhausted to waste.

Tunnels are quite commonly constructed in an arched back form instead of being flat. This is claimed to reduce trouble with papers likely to curl since the sheet breaks slightly over each support roll. Conveying the web in the tunnel has presented problems. Some installations rely on a felt or woven mesh to support the paper, but drying is retarded, as there is reduced circulation at the underside. When a bar or rod conveyor is used, there must be a speed differential between the web and the supports, otherwise the pressure of air holds the web and trouble is caused by local overdrying with cockling, due to the tension, between the overdried strips.

With a dual coated web the method of conveying the wet sheet presents no problem, since it must of necessity be supported on air until dry enough. The balance of pressures between the support jets and air circulating on the top side presents many problems and is critical. When the sheet is dry enough to be supported without damage to the coating on the underside, it is passed from the chamber over a suction device and transferred to a rod conveyor.

On those machines needing two coating heads to coat the two sides, it is usual to have separate tunnels, one above the other in the same structure. This economizes in space and construction costs.

Other installations utilize the space above the tunnel dryer for conditioning. Sections are separated and conditions are automatically controlled for temperature and humidity so that the paperboard is in ideal condition for calendering.

In the drying of fluid coatings there is a trend towards the use of combination equipment to utilize the best features of the various systems. The use of infrared drying is growing as it is being positioned within dryer systems to produce an improved drying condition.

4.14 board mill coating installations

4.14.1 Coated wood pulp board grades

4.14.1.1 AMERICAN MILL

An advanced on-machine coating installation in the USA is operating with three coating stations. It is producing coated board for food packaging, folding carton grades and base stock for hot melt coating, using 100%

virgin bleached kraft pulp furnish. A high proportion of hardwood pulp is blended with pine pulp to produce the desired bulk and surface smoothness for best print reception. The basis weight range is 160–600 g/m². Coating speed exceeds 210 m/min (700 ft/min).

The arrangement includes a Champflex coater at the first station. Either a metering bar, or a blade, can be used for smoothing off the excess colour. Here the wire side of the sheet is coated with a normal coating weight application 3–6·5 g/m². Drying is by high velocity air cap.

The second coating station is a controlled fountain blade unit, equipped with two blades for running in either direction (which depends on which side of the sheet coating is desired). Here some 9·5 g/m² can be applied per side at speeds upwards of 300 m/min (1,000 ft/min). Solids content is about 58% and usual weight application is 3–6·5 g/m². A 20:1 colour circulation is maintained. Drying is by infrared gas dryers used in the first and third drying zones, with a high velocity air unit (Fig. 4.14) situated in between.

The third coating station is airknife, used for coating the wire side of the sheet only. The unit applies up to 14 g/m² coating at 45% solids, av. 6·5–9·5 g/m². Drying follows in four drying zones. These are: infrared; medium velocity hot air; infrared: medium velocity hot air. Infrared is claimed to provide improved drying efficiency after the airknife, resulting in more uniform drying with elimination of coating "case hardening".

4.14.1.2 EUROPEAN MILL

The coating arrangement described concerns a Swedish board mill operating an on-machine controlled fountain blade coater and a fountain

Figure 4.15. COMMERCIAL ON-MACHINE COATING LINE
Close-up of blade and airknife coating stations operating on this machine are seen in Figs. 4.5 and 4.13.

airknife coater to apply coatings to the bottom side of Inverform made board, thereby meeting the requirements of high quality consumer packaging.

The coating units are designed to apply coatings up to a maximum speed of 274 mm (900 ft²). Board grades of up to 0·051 mm (0·021 in) and ranging from 40–80 lb/1,000 ft² may be either single- or double-coated on the bottom side. The entire coating line is under automatic constant tension control, with tensions ranging from four to twelve pounds per inch of width.

The sheet on the paperboard machine goes to a controlled fountain blade coater, which applies the first clay coating. Pigments used in the precoating include china clay and calcium carbonate. The adhesive formulation for the precoat consists mainly of protein and latex. The precoating is done at 56–58% solids and a coat weight of four pounds per 3,000 square feet. The coating is applied to the sheet by a fountain assembly consisting of a pipe and slotted applicator bar mounted on a heavy beam.

Excess coating is applied by the coating fountain to the web, the excess being metered off by means of a blade. From here the coated web passes over tension rolls and into a second coating station. This is an airknife arrangement. The coating colour used at the air doctor coater station is also water based and formulated from china coating clay, calcium carbonate, protein and latices. The top coat is normally applied at about 40% solids. Coating weights of up to eight pounds per 3,000 square feet are applied at the air doctor coater station.

The most unusual feature of the air doctor coater station is the use of the Controlled Fountain applicator to apply a smooth and controlled excess of coating to the web.

A 32 cm diameter, chrome plated tubular steel flutter roll is used after the airknife to lead the coated sheet into an air dryer. The air dryer consists of two sections of infrared heat followed by forty feet of air drying.

Moisture is added to the uncoated side of the sheet to control curl in the board. The principle of operation is a squeeze metering application. The moisturized board then passes over two 154 cm diameter dryer drums and a third tension sensing roll to the Kusters calender. The Kusters calender is complete with a swimming roll for crown control.

A brush polisher is used to obtain the desired surface finish characteristics on the coated sheet.

4.14.2 Coated "waste" board grades

An on-machine three station coating installation in Europe is producing a broad range of coated and uncoated paperboards from virtually 100% wastepaper furnish. The mill uses the maximum amount of *unsorted* waste and upgrades the product with extensive coating and finishing techniques.

Board machine capacity is 135–165 m/tons/day. Machine width is 2·9 m. Basis weight range is 250–800 g/m². Coating arrangement includes: two metering bar coaters; a roll coater; an airknife; gas fired infrared drying; and a high gloss process.

A feature of the high gloss process is that the coating is almost dry as it goes to the gloss calender. Other high gloss arrangements are run wet-on-wet onto the cylinder. Swimming rolls at top and bottom of the high gloss calender press the coated web at high pressure against the hot cylinder. A particular advantage of this arrangement is that the board machine can be run faster, in this case up to 65 m/min. Previous high gloss processes are reportedly limited to around 30 m/min.

Specific paperboard grades produced at the mill are:

Group I grades—bleached pulp lined (mostly face-lined); coated; for postcards, record jackets, cigarette and prestige packaging.

Group II grades (normal European, duplex board) bleached pulp face, de-inked waste middle, sorted waste back. All boards are coated for use as soap packets and in food packaging.

Group III grades—sorted waste face (kraft and sack waste), standard coated without high gloss.

references

1 KELLICUTT, K. Q., "Compressive Strength of Paperboard": *Fibre Containers*, Vol. 44, (5), 65, 1959.

2 MALTENFORT, G. G., "Freight Rule Requirements and Packaging Specifications"; *Paperboard Packaging*, (7) 152–162, 1964.

3 HIGHAM, R. A., "Call for Change in Liner Weights": *European Board Markets Supplement*, January 24, 1968.

4 BETTENDORF, H. J., "Proposed International Metrication of Linerboard Substances": *Paperboard Packaging*, (1969), 2, 39–43.

5 RANGER, A. E., "Evaluation of Fibrous Materials for Boardmaking and Converting": *Paper Technology*, 8 (3) 1967, 245:9.

6 STEENBERG, B., "Comparisons between Different Materials for Rigid Packs": *Swedish Pulp and Paper Assn. Information Sheet*, June, 1968.

7 HINE, D. J., "Influence of Finishing and Converting on Plybond Strength": 12th EUCEPA Congress 1968.

8 HINE, D. J., "Research and the Carton Maker": *PATRA Memoirs* 8, 1965.

9 KINGSNORTH, S. W., "Materials and Design–Carton Board Developments": Cartonex '67 conference, London.

10 *Paperboard Packaging*, 48 (7), 45, 1963.

11 MUNDAY, F. D., "The Effects of Printing and Converting Stresses on the Properties of Boards": 12 EUCEPA Congress, April, 1969.

12 KROESCHELL, W. O. and WYNN, C. A., "New Instrumentation for the Measurement of the Ply Bond Strength of Paperboard": 17th TAPPI Testing Conference, Sept. 1966.

13 BRIDGER, F. A. and MUNDAY, F. D., "The Relationship between Cartonboard, Bulge and Stiffness": *Paper Technology*, 10(2) 1969, 109:115.

14 HINE, D., "Material Testing and the Production of Folding Cartons": ECMA Congress, April, 1965.

15 MALTENFORT, G. G., "The Box Compression Test: Very Useful, but . . .": *Paperboard Packaging* 48 (1964) 56.

16 MALTENFORT, G., "Compression Strength of Double Wall Corrugated Containers": *Fibre Containers*, Vol. 43, Nos, 3, 4, 6, 7, 1958.

17 McKEE, R. C., *et al.*, "Compression Strength Formula for Corrugated Boxes": *Paperboard Packaging*, 48 (1963) 8:149.

18 BUCHANAN, J. S. *et al.*, "Combined Board Characteristics that determine Box Performance": *Paperboard Packaging*, 1964, 74–84.

19 BERGSTROM, J., "Properties of Corrugating and its Components determining Compression Strength of Boxes": FEFCO *Proceedings*, 1964, 25–32.

20 LANGAARD, O., "Optimisation of Corrugated Board Construction with Regard to Compression Resistance of Boxes": *The Billerud Flute Review*, 1968.

21 RANGER, A. E., "The Compression Strength of Corrugated Fibreboard Cases and Sleeves": *Paper Technology*, I (1960) 5:53.

22 KELLICUTT, K. Q., "Structural Design Notes for Corrugated Containers: Flat Crush of Corrugated Board": *Package Engineering* (10), 1959.

23 NORDMAN, L., "Research Work with the Pilot Corrugator at the Finnish Pulp and Paper Research Institute": FEFCO Congress, April, 1966.

24 ANGELL, B. S. and PASLAY, P. R., "Determination of the Stacking Strength of Corrugated Fibreboard Containers": *Proceedings of the Society of Experimental Stress Analysis*. Vol. 16, No.1, 109, 1958.

25 NORDMAN, L. and TORDI, M., "The Influence of the Components of Corrugated Board on the Stiffness and Strength Properties": FEFCO Congress, May, 1968.

26 HIGHAM, R. A., "New Corrugated Construction": *European Board Markets*, Vol. 5, (10), 1969.

27 GARTAGINIS, P. A. and OSTROWSKI, H. J., "Variables affecting the Converting Efficiency of Corrugated Combined Board and their Measurement": TAPPI 18th Testing Conference, September, 1968.

28 McKEE, R. C., *et al.*, "Properties of Corrugating Medium which Influence Runnability": TAPPI 50 (7) 35A–40A, 1967.

29 SIMMONDS, F. A., "Fluting Media Runnability and Microscopy Report": Aug. 1969, Forest Products Laboratory, Forest Service, U.S. Department of Agriculture.

30 BUCHANAN, J. S., "Stiffness—its Importance and its Attainment": 12 EUCEPA Congress, April, 1968.

31 RANGER, A. E., "Flexural Stiffness of Multi-ply Boxboard": *Paper Technology* 8 (1) 1967, 51:56.

index